Being Where You Are

By Stacey Thacker

"This little book shares huge, profound truths of our God. Beautifully encouraging for anyone in any challenging season of life."

Lara Williams, Author "To Walk or Stay"

"Being OK with Where You Are" is a beautiful, authentic, inspired book that walks readers from "not OK" to "OK" through real life examples, delightful stories, and honest dialogue. It is a journey of hope, challenge, and inspiration that anyone, in any season, would benefit from reading."

Crystal Stine, (in)courage Community Leader Coordinator

"I loved how Stacey made my not-so-normal feel very normal, all the while leading me higher …to Him."

Sara Hagerty, Writer, "Every Bitter Thing is Sweet"

"Being OK With Where You Are" is a breath of fresh air for those who are tired and worn thin. {Like me.} It reminded me of the sweet truth that where I am is both enough and not enough. Enough to do and be who God intends for this day … not enough to settle here for eternity."

Teri Lynne Underwood, Author, "Parenting from the Overflow"

"In reading this part of Stacey's journey, you will quickly

identify areas in your own life where you are not OK and learn how to begin walking the road of contentment, even if "where you are" does not change."

Gretchen Scoleri, Priority Associates

"This book is a deep breath amidst the crazy of our lives. If you've ever been broken or felt like you didn't measure up, this book will encourage and comfort you. It's as if Stacey is saying over milkshakes, "Where you are right now is OK. Really."

Kaitlyn Bouchillon, (in)courage Social Media (in)tern

"At the heart of our difficulties with being OK with where we are is this question: "If God never answered another prayer for us, would the knowledge of His gift of salvation be enough to convince us of His love and give us faith enough to trust Him no matter what?" It's a hard question to answer, but in her newest book, *Being OK With Where You Are*, Stacey Thacker masterfully teaches us the answer by comparing the heart issues we all deal with from time-to-time to real people of the Bible who struggled the same ways we do. And in the end, Stacey helps us see that being where we are is really the best place to be after all."

Brooke McGlothlin, Co-founder and Creator of The MOB Society (FOR moms of boys, BY moms of boys), and Co-author of Hope for the Weary Mom: Where God Meets You in Your Mess

Contents

INTRODUCTION

Jordyn Wieber's dream of an Olympic gold medal in the gymnastic all-around slipped through her chalked fingertips during the London 2012 games in a matter of minutes and by fractions of a point. We all felt the agony of defeat as we watched her, visibly shaken take a moment in disbelief to gather herself. Later, she spoke graciously of the tough competition and how proud she was of her American teammates during her post-meet interview. Eventually we saw what this champion was made of when she led her USA team to Olympic gold in the team finals. I think we all cried right along with her mom. The thrill of victory is even sweeter when the agony of defeat is still so vivid in our minds.

I love this story because it is just like real life. Dreams that slip away hurt like crazy. The pain is real. Sometimes we have to pull ourselves together and cheer others on as they go for the gold we were hoping to capture. Life doesn't always go the way we want; we have to decide in these defining moments if we are going to crumble or not.

I know this feeling all too well. Recently, I had an Olympic-sized disappointment of my own. Something I had been working hard on for months fell through my fingertips. I could almost hear the gasp of the crowd in my ears as my own dream died in the form of a short email. I took a moment to dance with the disappointment and then I had a decision to make. What next?

The Lord has a funny way of working in my life. While I was moving through my routine earlier that day, He whispered a blog title to me called "How to Really Be OK with Where You Are." I even wrote it down. Not two hours later I had my I'm not really OK with where I am moment and a perfect situation for working out my words.

This was not an unfamiliar place for me. In my forty-plus years I have had many disappointments. Some were small, others were life-changing. I thought back on each of those times in my life and saw a theme. For the first time, I realized learning to be OK with where you are is a process.

Confession time: I hate process.

I'm not entirely on the other side of it. But that is just fine. This book is my way of walking through it by faith with the Lord leading me every step of the way. I love that you are here. I'm secretly hoping we can work out *being OK with where we are* together.

I promise to cheer loudly for you. I'm hoping you'll cheer for me, too.

Looking forward,

Stacey

P.S. I have included a section called "Traveling Mercies" at the end of each chapter. You will find:

1. A Truth from God's Word.

2. A quote from the chapter to Think about more in depth.

3. A couple of questions to Talk over with friends.

Feel free to use this for personal reflection and as a journaling prompt. I pray this will allow you to take a moment and hear what God is speaking to your heart! I think this would also work well for small group discussion around a table with a few friends. Please know, my sweet sister, I have been praying for you and your journey.

I Admit it

〰️

I've never been a runner. There was one time in college when I tried to become one because I desperately needed to shed the freshman fifteen. My roommate Nichole loved to run. She ran for the sheer fun of it. I was pretty sure I didn't, remembering my days on the high school volleyball team. But, I needed results and fast. So I asked her to help me. She took on the challenge with great delight.

We would run after class just before dinner. Up hills and down, I felt every pound of the pavement on my entire body. She glided effortlessly beside me while I gasped for air. After our run she would say, "Wow, that was great!" and then proceed to make and eat the biggest plate of pasta I have ever seen. I wanted to die and eat a pint of ice cream. I'm pretty sure I whined about it to everyone who would listen. One day while running it occurred to me, "I hate this. I hate everything about it. So why am I doing it?"

I quit running that day.

Nichole went on to run marathons and mini-marathons. She simply loved to run. I did not. The day I admitted I was not a runner was the end of my running career, but it was the beginning of something else. I started walking instead. Walking worked for me. I could walk for miles without hurting. My mind was able to slow and could release the frustrations of my day or casually communicate with whoever might be with me at the time. Usually, this was just me and Jesus. As it turns out, He likes walking too.

Sometimes trying to be OK with where you are feels like running when you hate it. You gasp for air and all you really want to do is stop the madness. You might also be steadily whining about it to everyone around you. Consider this your permission slip to admit it and stop running around and pretending you are OK.

It is OK to admit it to yourself and God. Don't worry, He can take it. You'll feel better, too. It will also be the first step in your new journey. This new journey will take you straight to the heart of God. If you let Him lead the way, you will find you are not only OK with where you are, you are grateful for how you arrived.

I know first steps can be the most difficult. Wouldn't it be great if we could watch someone else go through the process ahead of us? Well, luckily for us Scripture is packed full of examples, and I think I've found a few we can learn a thing or two from.

Jonah Was a Disappointed Man

He had a God-call on his life he did not like. Mainly because it involved a certain group of people who were in the habit of killing those they didn't much care for. God said, "Go," while Jonah said, "No," and took off running in the opposite direction. You may be familiar with the fact that his running landed him in the belly of a large fish for a few days.

Jonah Admitted He Was Not OK:

"I sank beneath the waves,

and the waters closed over me.

Seaweed wrapped itself around my head.

I sank down to the very roots of the mountains.

I was imprisoned in the earth,

whose gates lock shut forever.

But you, O Lord my God,

snatched me from the jaws of death!

As my life was slipping away,

I remembered the Lord.

And my earnest prayer went out to you

    in your holy Temple.

Those who worship false gods

    turn their backs on all God's mercies.

But I will offer sacrifices to you with songs of praise,

    and I will fulfill all my vows.

    For my salvation comes from the Lord alone."

(Jonah 2:5-9)

While he admitted he was not OK, Jonah also did something else very important. He remembered all that was right about God.

He hears our prayers from the belly of fish or from our bathroom floors.

He is holy.

He is true.

He is our salvation.

He met Jonah in his place of disappointment and discontent and rescued him.

"Then the Lord ordered the fish to spit Jonah out onto the beach."

(v. 10)

Jonah made a beeline for his God-call. Suddenly, his view of God and His plan was bigger than his narrow-eyed view of where he thought he should be.

If you are reading this, there is a good chance you are not feeling entirely great about where you are today. God understands and wants you to pour out your heart before Him like Jonah finally did from the inside of a big fish. After you admit you are not OK with where you are, remember what is right about God. Use Jonah's words if you are struggling to find your own. Say it out loud so you can hear yourself. This will encourage your heart, I promise.

Bathroom Floor or the Belly of the Whale

I feel at this point it is important to tell you I have had many admit-it moments in my life. I call them bathroom floor moments because instead of the belly of a whale, it usually happens on the cold tile floor behind a closed door. I find this probably as humbling as being in the belly of the whale. You can't get much lower than the bathroom floor. These moments have not been pretty, but they have been memorable.

A. W. Tozer says of this place:

"So we will be brought one by one to the testing place, and we may never know when we are there. At that testing place there will be no dozen possible choices for us—just one and an alternative—but our whole future will be conditioned by the choice we make." [1]

Sweet friend, consider this your testing place. You are here for a reason and today you have a choice to make. Will you admit it to God, or will you keep pushing down the feeling of not being OK with where you are? The good news is it really doesn't matter if *here* is the bathroom floor, the kitchen table, or something that looks a bit like Shamu the killer whale. The most important thing is that you and Jesus show up. You get it all out, off your chest, out of your heart, and for sure off your mind. Then you look up and see all the grace and love in the eyes of your Savior and He assures you, "Now let's get to work on the rest of the process."

Because for the first time in a really long time, you both agree you are not OK. Quit running already. Take a walk with Jesus. He is listening. Remember, the journey has only just begun.

Traveling Mercies for Chapter 1:

Truth:

> "As my life was slipping away,
> I remembered the Lord.
> And my earnest prayer went out to you
> in your holy Temple."

(Jonah 2:7)

Think:

"While he admitted he was not OK, he also did something else very important. He remembered all that was right about God."

Talk:

1. What area of your life have you been trying to be OK on your own without success?

2. God rescued Jonah after he admitted he was not OK. What would rescue look like for you?

3. If this is indeed your "testing place" are you ready to admit it and move forward with God?

2 Give it to God

❧

I really don't intend for this to feel like a ten step program to being OK with where you are. Most of the time I find myself going back and forth between the "steps" like a game of hopscotch. Some days, they happen simultaneously in my life. In general, you don't have to complete one to be ready to move ahead to another. You might think of *Being OK with Where You Are* as an abstract painting instead of a paint by number. It may get a bit messy at times, but in the end you still get a vivid and personal piece of art.

My hope is you feel the freedom to jump to a section that seems to be a sticking point for you. You have that option. This is absolutely true for all the chapters with one exception. Chapters 1 and 2 always go together—like ebony and ivory, Anne Shirley and Dianna Barry, or Bugs Bunny and the Road Runner. If you are willing to read and walk through chapter 1 you need to read and walk through chapter 2. You can't separate the two. You may pause, take a breath and brace yourself for chapter 2. This is totally fine with me. Please, by all means grab a cup of coffee or some chocolate because you just admitted you are not OK with where you are. This is huge. This is life changing. You should probably take a moment to prepare yourself, because chapter 2 may be the hardest one. I know it is for me.

What Happens When You Get Up Off the Bathroom Floor

Sadly, you can't stay on the bathroom floor forever. You have to get up for obvious reasons. Someone will probably need to use it eventually. If you are a mama like me, it is most definitely because someone needs you. Sometimes those people who need you will stick their tiny fingers under the door to see if they can touch you. Sometimes they will pass a note underneath that says they are sorry. You might laugh a little, but still contemplate staying put.

But when you finally get up from the bathroom floor, wipe your tears, and check yourself in the mirror, Jesus will ask you one question. It is vitally important to answer it before going to chapter 3, 6, or 8. His question will be this:

"Do you trust Me?"

If you are like me, this question will seem to echo off the walls of your bathroom and straight into your heart. It will linger in the place where you are not OK. You might even ignore it for a while. Sooner or later, you are going to have to give an answer. Hopefully, by the end of this chapter you'll be ready. Maybe what you need is a bit of inspiration.

If you love something set it free.

If it comes back to you it was yours.

If it doesn't it was never meant to be.

- Unknown

Do you remember this bit of wisdom from the 1980's? My dentist had a poster with these words written in fancy letters hanging from the ceiling. It depicted a beach scene with a girl in a flowing dress tossing a dove into the air. I guess she really loved that bird. I always wondered why she wanted to set free the thing she most loved. I was sure that dove was never coming back.

Lately, I feel like I am living in this tired poem, and giving my "it" to God is a bit like tossing that dove into the air. I know there are shades of truth here. I have to be willing to let go of what I was hoping like crazy was God's best for me. There is one major difference, however. When I give my "it" to God I am not setting it free to fly and let the universe decide to bring it back or not. Instead, I am surrendering my plans to a personal God who loves me and knows what is best for my heart.

"For I know the plans I have for you," says the Lord. "They are plans for good and not for disaster, to give you a future and a hope."

(Jeremiah 29:11)

The trouble comes when I have something I really want to fit in God's plan for my life; I tend to hold on like a toddler who doesn't want to share with her playmate. "Mine!" is a word I am all too familiar with in a house full of girls. It is next to impossible to unwrap my three-year-old's hands from a toy she thinks she deserves. Parenting 101 teaches you to not force the child's hand, but offer her something better.

Often, God will orchestrate my life in such a way I have no choice but to let go of my "it" because it is not part of His good plan for my life. His hand extends to me and He whispers, *"Dear one, if you keep holding on to that, you can't hold on to my hand. There simply isn't room for you to hold both."* Faith comes when I can't see what else He is holding in His other hand or where the plan will lead. It feels like giving it to God is letting it go. When really, it is about having a hand to grab, His, and readying my heart to receive what He wants to give me instead. I have to trust His plan is infinitely better. At the end of the day, it is really about surrender.

When Surrender Looks Like the WWF

According to Merriam-Webster's online dictionary the word surrender means:

Sur-ren-der: to yield to the power, control, or possession of another. [1]

I can tell you already I don't much like this word. I am what you might call a control freak. I used to think I was a perfectionist, but now well into my forties I have realized I don't want things to be perfect. I just want my things to go according to my plans.

Possible synonyms for surrender are: cede, cough up, deliver, give up, hand over, lay down, relinquish, render, turn in, turn over, or yield.

I think we get the idea that surrender is about coughing up control to another. It is about turning in the keys and yielding the power to another to drive our own lives. As believers in Christ, we are asked to give Him absolute control. For me, at times, this is more of a scene from a WWF match on pay per view.

In this corner is the completely out of shape know it all Sister Stacey (because that is the best wrestling name I can come up with) and the other corner is God who created the whole world and really does know it all and then some.

The wrestling match is really short lived. I think we both know who wins in the end. I'm grateful I'm not the only one standing in the ring in ridiculous shimmery spandex wondering what just happened when the bell rings. Jacob, he wrestled, too.

"This left Jacob all alone in the camp, and a

man came and wrestled with him until the
dawn began to break."

(Genesis 32:24)

Like Jacob, I often find myself wrestling with God
alone in the middle of the night, because I am unwilling to
surrender my version of how life should go. I beg Him to
bless me and my handwritten-ending to my story. It is as
though I'm handing Him the page to approve how I think
the story should go. I cry out, "Bless me, Bless me Lord."
Or rather, "Bless the way I think life should be."

God blessed Jacob, but marked him for life by giving
him a bum hip joint. He also changed Jacob's name to
Israel. It made an impression. In my own wrestling with
God, He often gives me a reminder of His almighty power
and perspective telling me "I AM, who I AM. I see further
down the road, in fact I see the whole picture. When you
trust Me, you get to walk with the One who sees the end
as the beginning."

I want to surrender before the wrestling. I want to be
in a place where I trust my sweet Lord without the struggle. Do you struggle, too? Can I tell you something about
surrender I've learned the hard way? It is so much better
when I just lean into His plan. In the end He may have
something better for me. Or, perhaps He simply wants
to better me through the process. The truth is, setting
our something free might mean if it came back to us, it
wouldn't recognize us. Goofy 1980s clichés don't work in

God's economy. He is doing a greater work worth so much more.

I recently came across this quote by C. S. Lewis from the book *Mere Christianity*:

> He warned people to count the cost before becoming Christians. **"Make no mistake," He says, "If you let me, I will make you perfect.** The moment you put yourself in my hands, that is what you are in for. Nothing less, or other, than that. You have free will, and of if you choose you can push Me away. But if you do not push me away, understand that I am going to see this job through. Whatever suffering it may cost you in your earthly life, whatever inconceivable purification it may cost you after death, whatever it costs Me, I will never rest, nor let you rest, until you are literally perfect— until my Father can say without reservation that He is well pleased with you, as He said He was well pleased with me. This I can do and will do. But I will not do anything less."[2]

You know what I'm beginning to think? I think learning to be OK with where we are, admitting our disappointment and giving it to God, sets us up to let Him do a work in our lives that in the end will result in us looking a whole lot more like Him. I am blown away He would go to such lengths to see it happen in my life. He is even willing to let me suffer through this, calling me to unwrap my little hands from something that must not be part of His perfect plan for me.

> "And so, dear brothers and sisters, I plead
> with you to give your bodies to God be-
> cause of all he has done for you. Let them
> be a living and holy sacrifice—the kind he
> will find acceptable. This is truly the way to
> worship him."
>
> *(Romans 12:1,2)*

Truthfully, while we are on the topic of surrender, this might be the best place just to lay it all down. Sometimes God moves us to a place of brokenness and asks a little more from us than we anticipated. See, He doesn't really want to know if we are willing to give Him our "it." What He wants to know on this heart journey is if we are willing to give Him our all.

What if I didn't resist Him, but began instead to welcome this kind of work? What if we, together, moved forward in the process and saw real change in our lives? What if giving it to God was sweet surrender and we waited with hopeful breath that He would do a glory work in our lives?

What if we started today and simply whispered a prayer like this:

"Lord, I invite You to do the work You want to do in my life today. I need your grace more than I know or can express right now. This broken place is tender to the touch and everything within me wants to struggle within your will. But today, I offer you my plan for your purpose. I surrender my hopes, dreams, and discouragements into your hands. With my tiny fragment of faith, I say to you, 'Lord I trust You,' not only with this one thing, but with my entire life."

Traveling Mercies for Chapter 2:

Truth:

> "And so, dear brothers and sisters, I plead
> with you to give your bodies to God be-
> cause of all he has done for you. Let them
> be a living and holy sacrifice—the kind he
> will find acceptable. This is truly the way to
> worship him."
>
> *(Romans 12:1,2)*

Think:

"I think learning to be OK with where we are, admitting
our disappointment and giving it to God, sets us up to let
Him do a work in our lives that in the end will result in us
looking a whole lot more like Him."

Talk:

1. Have you found yourself wrestling with God lately?

2. What is God asking you to surrender?

3. Are you willing, right now, to lean into His plan?
   What would this look like in your life?

3 REMOVING THE VEIL OF FINE

❧

You might be OK with telling God you are not OK. You may figure, He knows anyway. It isn't easy, but it makes good sense to be on the same page with the One who knows your heart from the inside out. David knew this truth, too:

> "O Eternal One, You have explored my
> heart and know exactly who I am; You even
> know the small details like when I take a
> seat and when I stand up again. Even when
> I am far away, You know what I'm thinking.
> You observe my wanderings and my sleep-
> ing, my waking and my dreaming, and You
> know everything I do in more detail than
> even I know. You know what I'm going to
> say long before I say it. It is true, Eternal

One, that You know everything and everyone."

(Psalm 139:1-4, The Voice Translation)

Did you catch that? The Eternal One, He knows everything. He knows more than we know. I find this comforting in every way. I can rest in this truth for days.

However, one thing not so comforting is the idea of
everyone else knowing the small details of my life. I would
rather keep my not-being-ok-with-where-I-am between
me and God. I know He can keep a good secret, but my
Facebook friends, might be another story. Plus, if I tell
them I'm not OK, they might reject me and call me crazy.

Emily Freeman writes about this so beautifully in
Graceful: Letting Go of the Try Hard Life:

"The fear of rejection drives me hard, eating away at my
courage. And so my love is cautious. My faith is timid. My
story is small. I long to be seen, but I feel safe when I'm
invisible. So I stay the good girl. And I hide,"[1]

This is the story of my life. I lived small and played the
good and fine girl part like a pro. I did not want others to
see my weariness, so I hid behind a veil of "Fine." About
two years ago, I finally stepped out from my favorite hiding
place and put it all in a book called *Hope for the Weary
Mom,* which I co-wrote with my friend Brooke McGlothlin. Here is a small part of what I wrote:

"I've pretty much fallen short in every category. I am tired and not really good for much right now. The trouble is, Lord, I need to be amazing and I'm fresh out of amazing. At least it sure feels that way. Lord, I'm dry. Empty. Hit the wall. I got nothing.

So what do you do when need to be amazing and you are fresh out? For a while, I pretended like everything was normal. I smiled and put on my M.A.C. under-eye cream and my Smashbox lip gloss and I covered up the broken and weary mom with a veil. *I hid behind fine.*

It was far from fine. I had waves of discouragement. In fact I swam in it. I wondered how in the world I was going to make it each day. And if I am being honest, I would go ahead and tell you, I had thoughts that scared me. I told no one." [2]

The strangest thing happened when I finally said it out loud and pulled back the veil of fine. No one ran away from me. No one pointed and laughed. Not one person shook her head and said, *"Well, I'm out of here."* In fact, the stunning part was that girls just like me came running toward me.

I've learned a thing or two during this experience. The first is that when we are winning and life looks good on the outside, people want to be *like us.* But, when we are honest and share our broken and disappointed places, others strongly connect *with us.* When we are strongly connected with others, we can find purpose in our struggles like never before. In this honest and connected place we also find a powerful pocket of influence.

I often wonder what might have happened had I not waved my little white flag and taken off my veil of fine. I could have done my business with the Lord and moved on. I could have chosen to keep walking and not invited others to join me in my own pursuit of hope. That would have been OK on many levels.

God had a different idea. He wanted to use my hidden place for His glory. When God nudged me to come out from my habit of hiding, He blessed me with a community of women drawn into my story. But first, He also met me in my mess. He didn't ask me to come out of hiding without Him:

"It has taken me forty years and four babies to finally get to this place. In particular, the last two years have not been easy. But they have been necessary. See, what I've been learning is that I am not the good mom I always wanted to be. I don't have it all together. I am instead a dependent mom who is learning to live honestly where she is. I am a veil-torn mom who sees that in order to bring me face to face with grace, I had to be brought low and to the end of myself. I am a weary mom, who is reaching out for hope, and holding on with both hands." [3]

Veils, Sister-wives, and the One Who Loves Us Truly, Madly, & Deeply

When I think of hiding and veils I think of Leah. She is

the poster-girl for hiding. Her story of hiding is found in Genesis chapter twenty-nine.

> "Now Laban had two daughters. The older daughter was named Leah, and the younger one was Rachel. There was no sparkle in Leah's eyes, but Rachel had a beautiful figure and a lovely face."

(verses 16-17)

I can see her trying to blend in, not rock the boat, and be the kind of girl who was OK with where she was. But the truth is there was no sparkle in her eyes. *She was not OK.*

> "Since Jacob was in love with Rachel, he told her father, 'I'll work for you for seven years if you'll give me Rachel, your younger daughter, as my wife.'
>
> So Laban invited everyone in the neighborhood and prepared a wedding feast. But that night, when it was dark, Laban took Leah to Jacob, and he slept with her."

(Genesis 29:18-23)

The girl without a sparkle in her eyes pretended to be the girl with the lovely face. She hid behind the veil and played the part. Now, I'm willing to entertain the fact that

Leah did not have a whole lot to say about the part she was asked to play. Scripture simply states the fact it happened, we don't know for sure. But, what I think might be possible is Leah was able to follow through with the plan because she had been hiding for years. This was all too familiar territory for her. "Live small, stay invisible, be the good girl who always does what you are told," she might have thought.

We see in the story of Leah how hiding can lead to a whole mess of trouble. One man, two women, and twelve children set the stage for massive sister-wives drama. It sounds to me more like a HBO series than a Bible story. I'm so glad God included this in His Word. Real women, who live real broken lives I can identify with, speak loudly to me, especially when I am not OK with where I am. My heart breaks for Leah. Does yours, too? Do you see yourself in her distant stare wondering what could have been?

Yet, even in her hiding we see a loving God who met her right where she was. He knew her hiding places. He saw the one Jacob did not love and chose to bless her. He brought her out of hiding into a beautiful story of legacy through her son Judah. One of my favorite books called *The Jesus Storybook Bible* adds this about the story of Leah:

"Now when Leah knew that God loved her, in her heart suddenly it didn't matter anymore whether her husband loved her the best, or if she was the prettiest. Someone had chosen her, someone did love her—with a Never Stopping, Never Giving Up, Unbreaking, Always and Forever Love." (p. 74)

You know, when Leah took off the veil of fine, I think she was smiling from ear to ear. God loved her and that would never change. This same love frees us, like Leah, to be drawn out of our hiding places, too. These places look a lot like Starbucks and Target or the fake smile we wear when we are really not OK but want everyone else to think we are. Guess what I found out in the middle of my hiding? Jesus goes to Starbucks and Target, too. He was waiting for me when I got there and every morning when I was faking fine, putting on the veil, and pretending like my world was all good. I realize now more than ever, God wants us to share our stories and help others to see we work from acceptance, not toward it.

Kids Will Play

When I was little, my big brother and I would play hide-and-seek with our neighbors every summer evening. Base was always their front porch. They had one hundred places to hide in their yard because they had massive pine trees that lined their property. I remember the hiding. The fear. My heart pounding. I hated hiding. But, I hated being alone and found even more.

I was the youngest, so often the oldest girl, Karol, would say, "Hey Stacey, you can hide with me if you want." Did I want? Oh yes! But the thing is, Karol knew if I hid out with her, we'd probably be found quicker. *I didn't do quiet very well.*

But sometimes, we'd escape the finding. She would grab

my hand, say, "Go!" and take off running. My little legs would try desperately to keep in step with hers. We would make it with only seconds to spare, and yell out "Home free!!" Victorious we'd collapse on the glider, and wait out the hot July night counting lightening bugs till someone else was found. Not us. Not this time. We were home free.

The Rest of the Story

The day before *Hope for the Weary Mom* released as an expanded edition, I was terrified. I knew at the time there was no turning back. My small story was about to get a lot bigger and the veil was coming off for good. But something inside me nudged me to step out in faith one more time.

Remember when I told you girls came running toward me and my story? Well, there wasn't one or two. The number of girls who raised their hands and said, "Me too," was in the thousands. I spent so much time hiding in the darkness alone. Finally running towards base and yelling "Home free!" called out so many other mamas to run home, too. Today, I am humbled and moved to tears by their stories. One mom wrote after reading our book:

"I found myself in tears not even half way through *Hope for the Weary Mom*. I've been the "mom at the spa" and the mom feeling like a failure amongst the living-room forts and dirty dishes. This book is a lifeline for all weary moms to grab hold of God's Word, and each other, where we can truly find His masterpiece in the mess."[4]

Other moms said, "How did you know what I was thinking? You wrote my story." I knew, because hiding and veils had become my way of living.

You know what? I'm finally done with grown-up hiding. Quite frankly, it takes too much energy. I have an idea— let's grab hands and run home together. Your story of weary may not be found in mothering, like mine. That is fine. I'm tossing the veil to the wind along the way once and for all and I'd love for you to join me. Home base is waiting and the light is on. The one who loves us truly, madly, deeply is calling us out into a beautiful story. Let's live it.

Traveling Mercies for Chapter 3:

Truth:

"O Eternal One, You have explored my
heart and know exactly who I am."

(Psalm 139:1, The Voice Translation)

Think:

"But, when we are honest and share our broken and
disappointed places, others strongly connect *with us.* When
we are strongly connected with others, we can find purpose
in our struggles like never before. In this honest and connected place we also find a powerful pocket of influence."

Talk:

1. What or where is your favorite hiding place?

2. How does the story of Leah speak to your heart?

3. How could God use your broken place for His
    glory?

4 THE "C" WORD

"Comparison is the death of joy."

~ *Mark Twain*

When you are not OK with where you are, it is likely your best friend is having the time of her life. Her prayers are being checked off with "yeses" in groups of ten. The sun is shining, her fortune cookie outlook is fantastic, and she is ten pounds lighter. Bless her heart, you love her but you are a bit bothered by it all. You will find yourself clapping courteously for her on the outside, while you shout on the inside, "It just isn't fair."

Nothing brings out the comparison monster quicker than admitting you are not OK with where you are. It is as though the enemy is crouched in the corner waiting to attack the moment you say it out loud. He is quick to show you, when you are in the midst of your struggle, how great everyone else seems to be doing. In fact, he takes great delight in parading in front of you the success stories of your closest friends as you sit rehearsing your latest dashed hope.

I remember a time in my life several years ago when I was not OK with where I was. I had admitted it to God. I had even shared with a couple of people. But, I was not ready to share it with the world. A few friends invited me to go out of town and I jumped at the chance to escape for a couple of days. As we drove, I sat in the back seat alone trying to get my mind out of the mess it was in.

The conversation in the front seat turned to light fare as we drove. They discussed everything from kids, vacations, and curtains. Of course, they didn't know I was hurting; I had not mentioned it. And honestly, these were the types of conversations I was hoping for on a weekend away. But, at the same time I kept thinking to myself, "I'm here with my back against the wall and the enemy is in hot pursuit, and they are talking about home decor." It was if the whole world was at Disney World and I was drowning in the ocean called fear. It didn't seem fair.

Nobody Loves Me, Everybody Hates Me

We are an all-girl household except for one very brave super-dad. We lean toward a flair for the dramatic. If there is one phrase I hear almost daily it is, "That isn't fair. Why did she get more than I did?" I tend to roll my eyes at this approach because I know good and well the accuser had her fair share. This approach rarely works for me. I tell my girls, "Life isn't fair. This is a great lesson to learn young." I also sound just like my mother when I say it. I want them to know, the sooner they realize there is no fair-o-meter hanging mysteriously in the sky, the better off they will be. They usually sulk off to their rooms and toss themselves on their beds in a heap of tears that would give Scarlet O'Hara a run for her money. They are convinced nobody loves them, everybody hates them, and they might as well stop living all together. *How could they when life just isn't fair?*

We grown-up girls feel it too. I have done my fair share of wailing on my bed. We desperately want life to be fair. And by fair, I mean we want our version of fair. We want things to go our way, on our schedule, with our people. If we are honest, at times we want God to be a good fairy who shows up with a magic wand. We want Him to turn our soot-covered rags into fairytale worthy ball gowns every single time we ask. And for once, we want it to be about us, not our sisters. You know what I've discovered? Bible girls felt it, too. Just ask Martha.

Mary and Martha and Throwing Your Sister Under the Bus

Martha was standing in the kitchen. Mary was at the feet of Jesus. One of them was not happy with where she was, or maybe she was not happy with where her sister was by comparison. Do you know the story?

"As Jesus and the disciples continued on

their way to Jerusalem, they came to a certain village where a woman named Martha welcomed him into her home. Her sister, Mary, sat at the Lord's feet, listening to what he taught. But Martha was distracted by the big dinner she was preparing. She came to Jesus and said, 'Lord, doesn't it seem unfair to you that my sister just sits here while I do all the work? Tell her to come and help me.'"

(Luke 10: 38-40)

This is a snapshot moment in the lives of two sisters. In it we find a house full of hungry people and Martha bearing the weight of feeding them all. She was frustrated. When we are not OK with where we are, tension rises. Can you feel it too in this story?

From Martha's view, she had the short end of the stick. She was quick to throw Mary under the bus because in her estimation, it was not fair she was doing all the work.

Where was Mary while Martha was in the kitchen? She was lounging at the feet of Jesus. Mary did not feel the tension. Martha was not having it. In comparing herself to Mary, any joy she may have had in serving Jesus died on the spot.

Let me tell you how this attitude plays out in my life. I am a homeschool mom to four vibrant girls. Three of my girls are students and my youngest has decided at age three to start second grade like her big sister. Charming, right? This year I am re-learning and teaching eighth, fifth, and second grade. My brain has only so much room and this week--I promise you--it has reached full learning capacity. On top of teaching, I try to do just enough laundry to keep us clothed. I also feed our family of six three semi-nutritional meals each day. Add to this craziness ballet, piano lessons, and church activities. I frequently meet myself coming and going! Most days, I count it an honor to have a front row seat to every detail of my girl's lives. I find joy in the sweet snuggles while reading and cheer them on when they finally understand a math problem. We love sleeping a little later, staying in our pajamas on slower days, and sneaking off to the pool when the other kids are at school. There is plenty of joy to go around when my heart is in the right place.

However, when my frustration level rises it is easy for me to find a Mary to compare myself to. My Mary is dropping her kids off at five-day school and running through Starbucks on her way to a Bible Study group that is rocking her world with Truth. Afterwards, she is having lunch with her sisters in Christ and grocery shopping alone. She might even have time for a power nap after she puts the groceries away. Have mercy, the girl naps during the day.

I should go ahead and tell you that I know my Mary does not exist. She is just too good to be true. But, it is easy for me to believe she is alive and well when my world is overrun with needy people who actually expect me to feed and teach them a thing or two every day.

My whine fest to Jesus sounds a whole lot like Martha. Life seems unfair and I am more than ready to tell Him what He needs to do to fix my stuff so the scales tip in my favor. So, if you want to, go ahead and slip my name right in the space below where you read what Jesus has to say to Martha. Because I promise you, it is for me, too.

But Jesus said:

> "Oh Martha, Martha, you are so anxious
> and concerned about a million details, but
> really only one thing matters. Mary has
> chosen that one thing, and I won't take it
> away from her."

(Luke 10:41–42, The Voice Translation)

I love how Jesus uses Martha's name twice to make sure He has her attention. I think He said it tenderly. I think He looked her straight in the eye. I think He was not so much excusing Mary but gently pulling Martha back to the one thing she was missing. While she was busy complaining about where she was and where Mary wasn't, she was missing Jesus. He was drawing her back to Himself.

God is saying this to us as well. "Girl, you are so anxious and concerned over your place in life, but only one thing matters." Do you hear Him? He is drawing us back to Himself. He is making a place at His feet for us. We will probably come to Him frustrated, anxious, and with our list of complaints. We may feel like He is holding out on us. We may tell Him it is not fair. The truth is, what He is offering is what really matters. It is a deeper relationship with Him. He is willing to use anything in our lives to accomplish this if we will let Him. The question is, will we take that seat? Will we go deeper with Him, or will we continue to look around at everyone else and want what they have?

The Thing About What They Have and What We Want

Last year I was thrilled to watch Anthony Evans, Jr., the son of pastor and Bible teacher Dr. Tony Evans, on the NBC talent show called *The Voice*. Are you familiar with the show format? Contestants sing for judges who have their backs turned to them. They are chosen when a judge turns their chair for them. Anthony was chosen by pop singer Christina Aguilera. Rightly so, he has an amazing voice. However, he was eliminated during the battle round by another contestant named Jesse Campbell.

The good thing about this elimination was it allowed him to be at my church for a *Deeper Still* event featuring his sister, Priscilla Shirer. She is also an amazing Bible teacher, like her father. Anthony led worship for us. He also told this story about his Voice experience:

"A lot of people said, 'Anthony, why did you not talk about your faith on the show? Why did you not tell about your love for Christ and passion for worship?' The truth is, I did. I did not hide my faith at all. But it was cut from the show. You have no idea what ended up on the editing room floor. They only showed you what they wanted to from my story."

So many times we see an edited version of the lives of those around us. When we are not OK with where we are it is easy to think everyone else is doing great. Actually, they may be giving us an edited version of their lives. Most people do this. We tend to only show people the highlights of our lives. You know the status updates well:

My kids are the best!

Look at the awards they won!

My husband made me coffee this morning. He is so sweet.

Look at our fabulous vacation.

We are a happy family all the time.

And you know, that stuff is all great and should be shared. But nobody really has a Facebook-perfect life all the time. We all struggle. Sister, I want you to know, even though it seems like you are the only one who is not OK right now, you are not. You know the woman at church who always says she is fine and has the best shoes and hair to match? She has a few clips on the editing room floor. And if she doesn't today, she probably will next week or next year. The thing is, you probably won't ever hear about it.

Comparison is a two headed monster. It keeps us in an ugly place and it makes us want what our sister has. If we want to grow through this process and find Jesus in the middle of it, we have to look to Him and not others. When we are in a place of struggle, we have to look ten times more to Christ and His Word. The bottom line is, though, you have to choose it.

Your Snapshot Moment and the Choice You Have

You have admitted you are not OK with where you are. You have told Jesus all about it. You have, probably surrendered it to God each day since you admitted it. Hopefully, you have felt the freedom to remove the veil of fine and let others see your story so they can watch God work in your life. But today, in this snapshot-moment of your life, you have a choice to make. You can stand in the kitchen with your hands on your hips like Martha and say, "It isn't fair where I am standing." You can also look around at the happy little lives of the masses of people and wonder why your trials seem so thick and your dreams have died. You can say out loud, "It isn't fair where she is standing."

Or you can choose to look at Jesus. Consider the choice He made, and move on with courage and purpose.

> "[L]et us run the race that we have to run with patience, our eyes fixed on Jesus the source and the goal of our faith. For he himself endured a cross and thought noth-

ing of its shame because of the joy he knew would follow his suffering; and he is now seated at the right hand of God's throne. Think constantly of him enduring all that sinful men could say against him and you will not lose your purpose or your courage."

(Hebrews 12:2-3, J.B. Phillips Translation)

It wasn't fair that Jesus died. It wasn't fair that He suffered. But, Jesus never said, "It isn't fair." He fixed His eyes on the joy set before Him which included our salvation. He saw the longer view. We can too, when think constantly of Him and all He endured on our behalf.

My oldest daughter once chimed in during one of our "it is not fair" conversations and said to her sister, "If life were fair, Jesus wouldn't have died on the cross. So if you think you want a fair world, remember, you have Jesus, not what you deserve. You should be glad life isn't fair." I was a little proud and a lot humbled.

See, life might not seem fair in this snapshot moment. But remember, we have Jesus. And that is so much better.

Traveling Mercies for Chapter 4:

Truth:

> "[L]et us run the race that we have to run
> with patience, our eyes fixed on Jesus the
> source and the goal of our faith. For he
> himself endured a cross and thought noth-
> ing of its shame because of the joy he knew
> would follow his suffering; and he is now
> seated at the right hand of God's throne."
>
> ***(Hebrews 12:2, J.B. Phillips Translation)***

Think:

"God is saying this to us as well. "Girl, you are so anxious and concerned over your place in life, but only one
thing matters." Do you hear Him? He is drawing us back
to Himself. He is making a place at His feet for us."

Talk:

1. Go ahead, be honest, have you noticed how great life
    seems to be going for everyone else?

2. Have you lost your joy in serving Jesus because
    you are frustrated with where you are compared to

everyone else?

3. Is Jesus gently pulling you back to the one thing you have been missing? What is that one thing?

5 STANDING ON THE PROMISES

❧

Chapter five feels like a shift in our journey of *Being OK with Where You Are*. God has been whispering to my heart now was the time for these words. This is going to be the place where we pick up speed, keep moving forward, and don't look back. So far, I've asked you to Admit It, Let It Go, Remove the Veil of Fine, and stop using the "C Word." Do you feel a little broken down? Are you ready for a breath of fresh air?

I'm praying this chapter will be a lifeline for you. Please highlight and dog ear these pages. Let the words sink down deep into the place where you really are not OK. Tell your heart, today is the day we are going to draw a line in the sand. We will not leave unchanged, God's Word will not allow it.

I want you to know the following words have been hard for me to write. Not because they are fancier than the others. They just mean so much to me. In fact, the week leading up to my writing time has been filled with petty life annoyances, which when all piled up leave me feeling disconnected and weary. So, what comes next, you must know, is straight from the heart of God.

I hope this chapter is your favorite because I'm writing about His Words, not my own. I want you to say, "Chapter five was the one I re-read and shared with my sisters." I want you to eat these words up. If you remember anything else from this book, please let it be chapter five.

When God Tosses You a Lifeline, Take It

I learned something last week while my girls were casually swimming at the pool. My three-year-old needed to use the little girl's room, so I took off her water wings for a minute to make the trip to the facilities easier. When we returned to the pool, both she and I forgot to put them back on. I walked back to my chair and she unknowingly went in the water without them. It only seemed like a second when I turned around and saw her struggling to get to the side of the pool. Luckily, my ten-year-old was near her, grabbed her, and pulled her to safety. It happened so quickly. She went from bouncing in the pool to quickly being in trouble.

On the other side of the pool, a certified lifeguard was conducting a water safety course for a group of boys who looked to be around twelve-years-old. How odd for them to be learning how to save someone and my struggling daughter was only a few feet from them. They had no idea.

After she was once again water-winged and I was sitting on the edge of the pool within two inches of her, I watched the class in action. One of the things I learned was when a person is in trouble and offered a lifeline, the lifeguard needs to say, "Take the ring." In fact, when the boys would practice this task, he made them say it over and over. "Take the ring." I suppose this is because the drowning person is so busy struggling, they don't see the lifeline being tossed their way.

When we are not OK with where we are, we struggle just like my three-year-old did in the water that day. Sometimes, it happens so quickly we don't even see it coming. One minute we are fine and the next minute we are in over our heads and doing our best to make it on our own strength. Other times, we find ourselves struggling for days or even weeks and we miss the lifeline God has given us. We miss Him because we are overwhelmed by life. All the while He is throwing us our lifeline and saying, "Take the ring." Gratefully, He is the ultimate lifeguard and keeps tossing it to us until we grab it.

God's Word Is Our Lifeline

Several years ago, I was sitting at a table waiting to sing with Travis Cottrell and Mandisa when God tossed me a particular lifeline for the second time. Beth Moore invited my church choir to sing during one of her live events. I was so excited, because it was Beth Moore for crying out loud. I love her so much and this was a golden opportunity. I guess I was one of the only ones to feel this way, because only two of our church choir members came to sing. Fortunately, we were also joined by the Second Baptist Church Choir. They were very excited Beth called and had several members in attendance. The other woman from my choir was Jeana, and since I sort of knew her, we sat together and swapped stories while we waited.

I hadn't been in town long, maybe about a year, and my heart was desperately lonely. I guess you could say I was not OK with where I was in the larger picture of things. I mean I was very much OK with singing with Travis and Mandisa and meeting Ms. Beth Moore. I was not OK with being alone in my newish city where making friends was tough on this Midwestern girl. Jeana was kind and for some reason I felt like I could pour out my pitiful tale of woe to her. She listened for a while and then leaned forward and said to me:

"What has God promised you?"

I sat back and thought about giving her an easy and obvious answer. When she leaned in and said it again using a bit different inflection:

"Stacey, what has God promised YOU?"

It was at this point I remembered the verse I had taped to my refrigerator door:

"Behold, I will do something new, Now it

will spring forth; will you not be aware of
it? I will even make a roadway in the wilderness, Rivers in the desert."

(Isaiah 43:19, NASB)

God tossed me a lifeline in this verse as we were packing
to move to Florida the year before. I knew it was a promise
for my heart. I believed it. But, somewhere in the process
of relocating and the struggles of day-to-day life, I forgot. I
would walk to the refrigerator, open it a million times each
day with my promise taped to the front, and forget to let it
be the balm my soul needed.

Jeana's question to me was another lifeline for me. God
used her to bring me to a powerful realization: I already
had all I needed to move forward and find my way with
Him. I had His Word. It was right in front of me every
day. Foolishly, I had been content to drown in my own
sea of misery instead of grabbing onto His lifeline. So, in
all grace, He tossed it to me once again and called to my
heart, "Stacey, take the ring."

For the next hour I sang my heart out with the Second
Baptist Choir, Jeana, Travis and Mandisa. I also sat and
listened to Beth teach from the Word. I left that day a different girl. I was determined to keep God's Word not only
in front of me, but in my heart as well.

How did I do this? I'll tell you that verse and I became
great friends. I memorized it frontwards and back. I talked
to God about it a lot. I shared it with friends. It became

my banner cry back to the One who made the promise mine in the first place.

He knew I was in a wilderness. (He knew right where I was.)

He knew I felt as though I was in the desert. (He understood my heart.)

His promise to me, BEFORE we moved, was to do a new thing.

He would be the One to do a new thing. (I didn't have to do it.)

The new thing would be a path straight through the wilderness of not being OK. (I just needed to follow.)

The promise was ahead of me. (Before)

The promise was with me. (With)

Would I choose to see the lifeline?

Yes, I would.

Is this your lifeline? Has God tossed it to you before? Would you do me a favor today, and grab on with both hands?

God's Word Is More Than a Book

I've had a Bible my whole life. I have studied it for years. But last summer I did something I have never done before. I read it cover to cover in eighty-eight days. It was not hard to do, but it did take a firm commitment. I read for about one hour each day, usually in the morning before my family woke up. I had an amazing group of online friends who read with me through a reading plan called *Bible in Ninety Days*.[1] We cheered for each other to keep going.

I've always known it to be good. But this epic story of God's grace pierced my heart and gave me a fresh glimpse of my redeemer, I had never seen before. He relentlessly pursues us. He doesn't have to. But He does. He loves us like no other. His patience astounds me. His story is for me.

"The best place to meet God is in His Word. We know He dwells there," Priscilla Shirer, *Going Beyond*, May 2012

I met Him fresh in the pages of His Word. Promise after promise came alive for my heart. I was reminded, once again, that His Word does not bend or break but it is living and active and able to move in and out of our lives. His Word is where hope is found. His Word is where He is found.

I love how *The Voice Translation* of the Bible puts it:

> "The word of God, you see, is alive and
> moving; sharper than a double-edged

sword; piercing the divide between soul and spirit, joints and marrow; able to judge the thoughts and will of the heart."

(Hebrews 4:12)

Remember in the last chapter when I said He is inviting us to a deeper relationship with Him? The reason He has a seat for us at His feet is because He wants to pour His Word into us. His truth will go to work on our hearts and actually do the surgery we need for the healing to begin.

Amy Carmichael once said, "There is always the word waiting in His Book, which will meet us where we are and carry us further on."[2] When we come to the Word of God, He meets us. His Word goes to work on our hearts to change us, and through this encouragement He will carry us further on. Do you need that today? Maybe you find yourself in place where you can't take another step. This is not a problem—He is prepared to carry you with the soul strengthening power of His Word.

He meets us in His Word.

He changes us.

His Word carries us further on.

We can be OK with where we are, starting today.

Just Focus on One Thing

To stand on the promises of God when the howling storms come, we have to know them. We need to have them handy, in our pockets to pull out when we need to be reminded. We need to scribble them on cards and tape them to the refrigerator. Or we need to go high tech and put them on our smart phone lock screens. The point is we can't stand on what we do not know.

Webster's Dictionary of 1828 defines the word stand like this:

stand: "to be fixed or steady; not to vacillate."[3]

God's promises are meant to fix and steady us. When I am not OK with where I am, my focus is on everything going on around me. My life is anything but steady. I'm easily overwhelmed because I have forgotten to focus on what truly matters—His still small voice.

This reminds me of my favorite scene from the newest "Superman" movie. In the movie, Clark Kent is coming to grips with his true identity. As a super man from another world, one of the things Clark struggles with is a keen awareness of his senses. He sees and hears every little detail in the world. At times, it overwhelms him.

His Kansas mother, played by Diane Lane, has taught him to focus on one thing when the world pushes and pulls him to the limit. During one scene, Clark has locked himself in a closet at school to escape. His mother comes running and bends down low and says in a soothing tone, "Just focus on one thing Clark." She continues, "Try focusing on the sound of my voice. Can you hear it, Clark?"

I know there are days you want to lock yourself in the closet and shut out the world, too. Sometimes it is all too much to take in. But, we have a loving Father in heaven Who is standing on the other side of the door saying, "Just focus on one thing today. Focus on the sound of My voice."

Guess what happens when we focus on His voice? Listen to what the prophet Isaiah says:

> "You will keep the peace, a perfect peace,
> for all who trust in You,
>   for those who dedicate their hearts
> *and minds* to You.
>
> So trust in the Eternal One forever, for He
> is like a great Rock—*strong, stable, trustworthy, and* lasting."

(Isaiah 26:403, The Voice Translation)

Can You hear your Father whispering this to you right now? It comes wrapped in the perfect peace your heart needs to be OK with where you are today, tomorrow, and next week.

When I'd Rather Stay in the Closet

When I have days I'd rather stay in the closet, I find a few promises my heart can cling to. I listen to the sound of His voice. Here are a few of my favorites:

1. I will never leave you nor forsake you. (Hebrews 13:5, ESV)

2. Jesus Christ is the same yesterday, today, and forever. (Hebrews 13:8)

3. The eyes of the Lord search the whole earth in order to strengthen those whose hearts are fully committed to him. (2 Chronicles 16:9a)

4. For I can do everything through Christ, who gives me strength. (Philippians 4:13)

5. If God is for us, who can ever be against us? (Romans 8:31)

6. And I am convinced that nothing can ever separate us from God's love. (Romans 8:38)

7. May the God of hope fill you with all joy and peace in believing, so that by the power of the Holy Spirit you may abound in hope. (Romans 15:13, ESV)

8. For we are the product of His hand, *heaven's poetry etched on lives,* created in the Anointed, Jesus, to accomplish the good works God arranged long ago. (Ephesians 2:10, The Voice Translation)

9. The grass withers and the flowers fade, but the word of our God stands forever. (Isaiah 40:8)

10. And I am sure of this, that he who began a good work in you will bring it to completion at the day of Jesus Christ. (Philippians 1:6, ESV)

3,573 Waiting for You

I read there are 3,573 promises in God's Word for you to pick from. You can look at the first one in Genesis 3:15 or the last one found in Revelation 22:20 or any of the other 3,571 in between. They are all there in black and white waiting for you and me to read. One promise that sums them all up nicely is found in 2 Corinthians 1:20:

"In Jesus we hear a resounding 'yes' to all of God's many promises. This is the reason we say 'Amen' to and through Jesus when giving glory to God." (The Voice Translation)

3,573 promises are all "Yes" in Jesus. Can you be OK with where you are today? Yes, you can. Because, Jesus who is the same yesterday, today, and tomorrow has a promise for you. You can grab onto it. It won't ever change. But if you stand on it, you just might.

So, sweet friend of mine, I have a question I would love to ask you:

What has God promised you?

Traveling Mercies for Chapter 5:

Truth:

"Behold, I will do something new, Now it will spring forth; will you not be aware of it? I will even make a roadway in the wilderness, Rivers in the desert."

(Isaiah 43:19, NASB)

Think:

"To stand on the promises of God when the howling storms come, we have to know them. We need to have them handy, in our pockets to pull out when we need to be reminded. We need to scribble them on cards and tape them to the refrigerator. Or we need to go high tech and put them on our smart phone lock screens. The point is we can't stand on what we do not know."

Talk:

1. What have you been focusing on lately that is overwhelming you?

2. How have you seen God's Word change you in the past?

3. What is one promise you can stand on today?

6 YOU MAY NEED A CHEERLEADER

❦

Give me an "e", give me an "n", give me a "c-o-u-r-a-g-e-m-e-n-t". What's it spell?

Encouragement.

Say it again.

Encouragement.

Why? Because you need it now more than you know. You have bravely walked toward being OK with where you are for the past few weeks. I'm so proud of you. But you still have days when you would like to toss this book across the room and quit. Lucky for you I have been there many times, and figured this day would come. Plus, as an added bonus, I spent years as a cheerleader and I know how to *pump up the jam*.

Ready, OK, with a Sprinkle of Mary Katherine Gallagher

I saw it in my daughter's eyes on Halloween night. She needed some encouragement, too. She was sitting in the middle of a mud puddle in a long, white, Princess Leia outfit, candy everywhere, water soaked and dirty. Quitting seemed like the obvious thing to do because let's face it, she was not OK with where she was. She was defeated and embarrassed.

"I want to go home," was all she said.

I didn't blame her. I wanted to go home, too.

But, I dug deep. I grabbed her with both hands and speaking my best life-giving words I said, "This is a one shot deal. I know you are upset. But tonight is the only night to do this. Now, your bucket is empty. Let's fill it again. Decide right now, to get up, and have some fun." I might have put my hands up in the air and assumed the "Superstar" position just to add an exclamation point on the end of my pep talk. If only Instagram were alive and well back then, we could have photographic proof.

To my surprise, she wiped her tears, turned around and headed to the next house. She told the next three people about her fall. They gave her twice the going trick-or-treat rate out of sympathy. She challenged herself to be brave and ended up with heaping amounts of sugar and chocolate as her reward. She skipped from house to house and proclaimed, "This is so much fun!"

I knew the years of cheerleading would not go to waste and this moment proved it. Standing on the street and seeing Princess Leia smiling in spite of her dirty bum, made me realize sometimes I need a cheerleader, too. I need her most when I'm sitting in a mess and my dreams are scattered around me soggy and wet. Don't we all?

Shake Your Pom Pons

When I think of cheerleaders I think of practicing at 6:00 AM on hot summer days, riding buses and cheering for the team rain or shine. I think of camp and spirit stick winning. I think of Bon Jovi singing "Living on a Prayer" and pep rallies. Mostly, I think of how much my heart loved those years. Contrary to what most people think of cheerleaders, it wasn't because I gloried in the popularity or the short skirts. I simply loved cheering. I loved the words, optimism, and heartbeat of it. I loved being for the team, wearing the school colors, and doing life together.

During my cheerleader days, the original "Friends" song by Michael W. Smith was popular. We sang it until we kind of sort of hated it. Sorry Michael, but I'm guessing you get that a lot.

Deep down, we know this song is true. We want friends who can see the dreams and hopes God has planted in our lives. We want them to believe it when we can't. We especially want friends to keep us close when we are not OK with where we are. We need friends who are the forever kind.

The best of friends are not only faithful, but serve as our own personal cheerleaders. They see the good when no one else does. They pick up their pom pons and shake them in our faces when we would rather just take a seat on the sidelines. They remind us who we are and how our dreams matter. They certainly can make a difference in your life when you not winning. And if they are in it for the long haul, they will stick around even when everyone else seems to be choosing other people for their star players.

Funny, though, it seems like when we find ourselves sitting in the puddle with Princess Leia, we often send our friends away. We think we are better off alone. God often breaks through and has other ideas, even when we are something akin to a Bitter Betty.

The Woman Whose Name was Bitter

If I didn't know any better, I would think this was a verse lifted straight from a country song:

> "But she said, "Don't call me Naomi; call
> me Bitter. The Strong One has dealt me a
> bitter blow. I left here full of life, and God

has brought me back with nothing but
the clothes on my back. Why would you
call me Naomi? God certainly doesn't. The
Strong One ruined me'."

(Ruth 1:20-21, The Message)

*Call me Bitter. I have come home with only the clothes on
my back. My life is ruined.*

It is safe to say, Naomi was not OK with where she
was, where she had been, and the prospects for her future.
She even went so far to change her name to the sound of
bitterness. Yeah, every time you call my name, be reminded
"I'm bitter." She wanted everyone to know what you hear
is what you get.

But was Naomi alone? Did she only come home with
the clothes on her back? Well, not according to this part of
the story:

"At this Orpah and Ruth wailed and wept
again. Then Orpah kissed Naomi, said
goodbye, and returned the way she had
come. Yet Ruth refused to let go of Naomi."

(Ruth 1:14, The Voice Translation)

Bitter came home with a daughter-in-law named Ruth
who refused to let her go. She stayed with a shell of woman who was not much fun to be around. Though pushed

away time and again, Ruth stood firm:

> "Stop pushing me away, insisting that I stop
> following you! Wherever you go, I will go.
>
> Wherever you live, I will live. Your people
> will be my people. Your God will be my
> God."

(Ruth 1:16, The Voice Translation)

This is beautiful, right? Guess what Bitter said? She said nothing more. She walked on home with a treasure of a friend beside her and when she arrived home told them she had nothing.

When your name is Bitter, you tend to see only what you don't have. She saw heartache, loss, and a long road home. Ruth stayed with Naomi when she was not invited or encouraged to do so. Ironically, the name Ruth means beloved. Bitter walked with Beloved and actually could not see her as a gift.

Judgments aside, I am more like Naomi than I care to admit. When I am hurting and overwhelmed, I withdraw. I hide. (Remember chapter 3 and The Veil of Fine?) My stress behavior, if you care to know, is to act as though I'm fine and at the same time cave far inside my own heart. During these times, it is hard for me to want people around, let alone be overjoyed when they declare their commitment to me. So, I get Ms. Bitter and her ways.

The story goes on to include a dashing kinsman redeemer (aka biblical version of the Bachelor) who eventually marries Ruth. Naomi is blessed with a son through the new couple. Insert, happily ever after here:

> "May this child give you new life. May he strengthen you and provide for you in your old age. Look at your daughter-in-law, Ruth. She loves you. This one devoted daughter is better to you than seven sons would be. She is the one who gave you this child. Then Naomi held the child tightly in her arms and cared for him."

(Ruth 4:15,16 The Voice Translation)

Here in the middle of Bitter's story is blessing. The real blessing comes through a relationship she tried to send away. How grateful she must have been when she held the baby in her arms and saw God's plan was to bless, and not to curse. He used a beloved girl named Ruth to bring blessing to one whose heart was almost dried up.

I love how when we are not OK, He pushes us on one step further with grace stories like the one of Naomi and Ruth. Better yet, He sends a Ruth to us in our own moment of crisis to walk with us when we think we would be better off alone.

A Modern Day Ruth

I was bitter. Yes, I'll admit it. I spent most of my days telling God I did not understand what He was doing or how He was going to use the mess we were in for my good and His glory. My bitterness was a deep pit and I was bathing in it daily. It was threatening to consume me.

My friend whose name is not Ruth was a safe person I could pour out my heart to over vanilla cupcakes and coffee. She listened and took me to the movies when I needed to get lost in another story.

I remember when she told me my pit did not have to define my life. It was not my life. It was only part of my life. Then she casually said,

"I signed you up for Bible study. It starts next month. You can sit by me."

I guess I believed on some level what Betsie Ten Boom said, "There is no pit so deep that He is not deeper still."[1] But in this one moment, my sweet friend grabbed a shovel and started to help dig me out one scoop at a time.

Every week I went to Bible study, my view of God grew. My friend kept shoveling, and by the end of the year I was in a much better place. Her willingness to walk with me was life changing. She did not take on the responsibility of fixing me or my problems, but she showed up with a shovel called commitment when it would have been easier to walk away.

A modern day Ruth does not have to do much for us to make a difference. She can extend a hand, buy us a cup of coffee, or wash our dishes while we hold our newborn baby. I have had a consistent stream of them come in and out of my life. Do you have one right now you have tried to send away? If you are not OK with where you are, chances are God has someone in mind who is willing to do a little shoveling in your life. Who comes to mind when you read that last sentence? Can you text or call her to meet you at Starbucks? I'm guessing, she will even buy.

Keep Calm and Find Your Exit Buddy

Remember when I told you this book is about process? I also told you I don't have a fondness for process. I confess I get stuck from time to time on a current of discouragement as I'm trying to move forward. I have found, on the stuck days, I need an exit buddy. I need a modern day Ruth to lock arms with me and help me to "Just keep swimming …"

In the movie *Finding Nemo*, Dory was the cheerleader Marlin didn't know he needed. I love the scene where the pair is on their way to rescue Nemo and they catch a ride on the East Australian Current. They are about to exit the current when a righteous dude of a sea turtle named Crush says,

Crush: "OK, first, find your exit buddy. Do you have your exit buddy?"

(Dory grabs Marlin and puts a suction-type hold on him).

Crush: "OK. Squirt here will now give you a rundown of proper exiting technique."

Squirt: "Good afternoon. We're gonna have a great jump today. OK, first crank a hard cutback as you hit the wall. There's a screaming bottom curve, so watch out. Remember: rip it, roll it, and punch it."[2]

God has always been a fan of the buddy system, too. Adam had Eve. *The animals came two by two.* David had Jonathan. Jesus had twelve men. Paul had Silas, Timothy, Barnabas, and Mark. We see this throughout His story of redemption.

> "And if one person is vulnerable to attack,
> two can drive the attacker away. As the
> saying goes, "A rope made of three strands
> is not quickly broken"

(Ecclesiastes 4:12, The Voice)

You were made like Him, and He is that perfect strand of three—Father, Son, and Holy Spirit. God wants you to know He made you to fit with others. Is today a day when you need an exit buddy? Someone to ride the current with you and remind you it is going to get better? The best of the best are those who share your heart and passion for Him. In fact, they may be who God sends to help drive away the doubts and discouragements you feel.

Help, I've Fallen and I Can't Find My Exit Buddy

"This sounds great on paper," you may be thinking. "But what about when there is no exit buddy to be found? What do you do then?" This is a great question. I want you to know these days are real. I have walked them. Not long after my friend signed me up for Bible study, I moved a thousand miles away. These were the lonely years God had planned to be part of my story. But, where loneliness lived, God and His Word entered in. I found a promise I was clinging to and going deeper with Him than I ever had. He was the ultimate exit buddy and ready to rip it and roll it every single day with me. He was the cheerleader my heart needed most, as every day He reminded me He was for me. My friendship with Him has never been sweeter.

Still, in those lonely days I asked God to send me friends who would be like sisters to me. He did that, in time, because Faithful is His name. He was also preparing my own heart for when He would bring new sister friends into my life. If you are wondering where you can find a beloved sister to walk with on the hard days, trust God will provide this for you. I'm believing this with you, because He has done so in my own lifetime and time again.

And for heaven's sake, if He sends you one, don't tell her your name is Bitter and try to ship her home. She is an answer to prayer, and you need to keep calm and swim on, together.

Traveling Mercies for Chapter 6:

Truth:

> "And if one person is vulnerable to attack, two can drive the attacker away. As the saying goes, "A rope made of three strands is not quickly broken"

(Ecclesiastes 4:12, The Voice)

Think:

"When your name is Bitter, you tend to see only what you don't have. She saw heartache, loss, and a long road home. Ruth stayed with Naomi when she was not invited or encouraged to do so. Ironically, the name Ruth means beloved. Bitter walked with Beloved and actually could not see her as a gift."

Talk:

1. Why do we send our cheerleaders away when we need them most?

2. Naomi could not see the blessing right in front of her because of her own bitterness. Who has God has placed in your life who might be a blessing for you?

3. A Modern Day Ruth does not have to do much to encourage us. How has a friend locked arms with you in the past and helped you get unstuck? (Extra:Send her a note to say thank you!)

7 ON PRUNING

❦

Pruning is a deeply personal story. These words are my heart-laid-bare and not easy to write. I wish I could skip this chapter all together. But I know you are here because you desire to keep moving one step at a time toward being OK with where you are. This part can't be avoided. It reminds me of *Going on a Bear Hunt* by Michael Rosen. Have you read this life lesson wrapped up in a children's storybook?

"You can't go over it.

You can't go under it.

You have to go through it."[1]

There is simply no way to go over, under, or around the subject of pruning. We will, at some point, have to go through it. Let's go through it together, shall we?

Pretty Little Liars

The Liars Bench sat outside Rice's Bait Shop and across the street from the little Baptist church I grew up in. We would sneak over between Sunday school and church to buy candy and Chocola. By the way, I'm pretty sure nothing tastes better than an ice cold Chocola on a hot summer day. I sat on that bench every Sunday, rain or shine in my black Mary Jane shoes and tried hard not to spill my drink on my dress. I may have also told some little white lies as well.

If you and I could sit together on the Liar's Bench drinking our cold, chocolatey goodness, I would look you straight in the eyes and say:

"Pruning doesn't hurt one bit."

Of course, I'd be lying if I did. But, we'd be sitting on the bench and that would make it all right. Or I could open the pages of my journal and tell you the truth:

"Here we are again.

I'm broken to pieces.

In this one area you have elected to take Your pruning sheers and cut back to the deep. It is in this pruned place I am vulnerable. Over and over again I have laid it down. It is yours Lord. You know best.

Some days, I am weak and You are strong.

Some days I am just weak.

I don't know why this one thing is so hard. Why it hurts so bad. Why the longing is more than I can bear. So, here is my plea. 'Take it. If it's not to be, and perhaps it never will, then please take away the desire. Make me indifferent. Fill that space of want only with YOU and what YOU want for me.' That's it. That is all I have.

The lies are subtle. I am quick to believe them more than not. I have so many promises stored up in my heart, but in this one area, the arrows go straight to the heart. I am defenseless.

No good.

Discarded.

Forgotten.

So not true. I know, I know, I know. But I feel it to the very center of who I am."

Pruning hurts. And that is the honest to goodness truth.

We Are All Good Pruning Material

Every living thing is pruned in some way. According to Webster's Dictionary of 1828, to prune means:

Prune: "To lop or cut off the superfluous branches of

trees, to make them bear better fruit or grow higher, or to give them a more handsome and regular appearance."[2]

Wikipedia says the reasons to prune plants include:

"deadwood removal, shaping (by controlling or directing growth), improving or maintaining health, reducing risk from falling branches, preparing nursery specimens for transplanting, and both harvesting and increasing the yield or quality of flowers or fruits."[3]

Jesus ties it into our spiritual life here by saying:

"I am the true vine, and my Father is the gardener. He cuts off every branch in me that bears no fruit, while every branch that does bear fruit he prunes so that it will be even more fruitful."

(John 15:1-2)

First, God prunes where spiritual decay or disease has settled into our lives. It could be a place where pride moved in and set up shop, no longer bringing glory to the Lord. Or it is a nonbearing fruit superfluous branch. So, He cuts it away.

The second place God prunes is an area bearing a good harvest of fruit. This type of pruning usually catches us off guard and in particular may be the very reason you are reading this book. God cut away something in your life you loved, and you are not OK with it.

When God prunes disease out of our hearts, we may grumble, but we realize it is for our good in the long run. The second type of pruning requires a greater trust, I believe. It is in this pruning place we are left to wrestle with God, finding it hard to believe He really has our best in mind. I struggled with this pruning for years, and   words scribbled in my journal show it:

"I can't even begin to put into words what my heart is feeling. I have prayed, secret prayers for so long. No one has known the depth of my waiting. Tears have fallen many times. And sometimes, I was just too broken to even produce tears."

Pruning breaks and cuts us. It wounds us and leaves us open and vulnerable. Pruning is death and life all mixed up together. It is a walk through Galatians 2:20:

> "I have been crucified with Christ. It is no longer I who live, but Christ who lives in me. And the life I now live in the flesh I live by faith in the Son of God, who loved me and gave himself for me"

(ESV)

A. W. Tozer says it best, I think. So I'll borrow his words:

"It is never fun to die. To rip through the dear and tender stuff of which life is made can never be anything but deeply painful. Yet that is what the cross did to Jesus and it is what the cross would do to every man to set him free."[4]

The path of being OK with where you are often involves pruning, and pruning passes through the heart of the Gospel. *Out of death, comes life.* The death of Christ purchased my redemption, and I am called to be like Him:

"When my flesh yearns for some prohibited thing, I must die. When called to do something I don't want to do, I must die. When I wish to be selfish and serve no one, I must die. *When shattered by hardship that I despise, I must die.* When wanting to cling to wrong done to me, I must die. When enticed by allurements of the world, I must die. When wishing to keep besetting sins a secret, I must die. When wants that are borderline needs are left unmet, I must die. *When dreams that are good seem shoved aside, I must die."* Milton Vincent, *A Gospel Primer*, p.41 (emphasis mine).

Hardships? Check. Wrong done to me? Check. Dreams shoved aside? Check. Are you having fun yet? We are all good pruning material and that means we are pretty much dying all day long. That Liars Bench is looking like a pretty sweet spot right now, isn't it? Ah, if only, right? The good news is, God has his hands all over us, and if we are patient, the master gardener will do a beautiful work.

The work of pruning is not to hurt us maliciously,

but to change our growth patterns and produce more fruitful branches.

But Wait, There Is More

One of my favorite writers is Elisabeth Elliot. She says on the subject of pruning:

"This is a painful process. Jesus knew that His disciples would face much suffering. He showed them, in this beautiful metaphor, that it was not for nothing. Only the well-pruned vine bears the best fruit. They could take comfort in knowing that the pruning proved they were neither barren or withered, for in that case they would simply be burned up in the brushpile."[5]

Take a deep breath with me and repeat Elisabeth's words:

It is not for nothing.

Pruning serves a purpose in our lives. He would not bother with us if we were meant for the brushpile. Are you well-pruned? Then watch out, because in time you will bear much fruit, *because it is not for nothing.*

When my girls were younger I took them to a beautiful flower garden located in our home town. The rose bushes were bursting with gorgeous full blooms and we could not believe the variety and colors of each kind.

The gardener came by and offered them each a flower from their favorite bush. He said, "It is good thing you are here today, because tomorrow we will be cutting them back to the stem." We were shocked. Why on earth would he cut away such beauty? The answer was simple. Pruning them would grow bigger and more beautiful flowers during the next blooming season. The experts knew exactly what they were doing.

I don't know how it all works, why the pruned place produces more fruit. But it does. I have experienced it in my own life. Years ago, my husband and I were serving in full-time ministry, walking in close step with the Lord, and following His path. When suddenly, we found ourselves in a pruned place that included letting go of our ministry dream, our home, our community, and our extended family.

He not only pruned us, He transplanted us. He took the cutting and planted us in fresh soil of a new town. I felt bruised, small, and insignificant. By His grace and tender care the transplanted vine began to grow. Our hearts were deeply trusting and abiding in Him. The empty space where He cut away those other good things, became a place He was allowed to enter into Himself. The growth that occurred as a result of this pruning was far greater than it would have been if we had been left alone.

I remember a song that gripped my heart during this time by Ginny Owens. It was called "If You Want Me To" and I sang it often in those days because I needed to tell Him how hard it was. I needed Him to remind me that my trials brought me closer to His side. In the song she talks about broken pathways and unclear signs. If Being OK with Where You Are had a theme song, this would probably be it.[6]

We wouldn't choose the pruning if someone paid us. But He promises we are never alone. Think back to the beginning of your pruning. Are you who you were when you started this journey? No, I'm pretty sure you are not. You have been changed. Do you see it?

He also promises this as well:

> "By this my Father is glorified, that you bear much fruit and so prove to be my disciples"

(John 15:8 ESV)

Our broken and pruned places not only bear greater fruit, but bring the Father glory. This is what it is all about. We press deep into Him, and through us He does a work that brings glory to His name. Now that is something worth singing about.

The Beautiful By-product of the Pruned Life

The beautiful by-product of your pruned place is it has value to others. If you have removed the veil of fine and opened your story for others to see, they will benefit from your journey. Our humbled position has the unique ability to speak powerfully to another soul when we do not hide the work God does in our lives.

My pruned places have become a hot bed of ministry. This is because pruning allows us to have a perspective we would not have otherwise. Of course, this perspective takes time and the truth is every pruning cycle is different. For some it may be weeks or months. I know in my life, the pruning has at times lasted for years. I don't tell you this to discourage you. Honestly, I see it as a greater work God saw fit to do in my life. There was no other way for me to learn of His grace and love for me. I needed this heart surgery. In the process, my ability to minister to hurting women was cultivated as well.

When you share the place that humbles you, people tend to listen. But first, you have to be willing to tell others about it. Are you ready, my friend, to see a beautiful by-product emerge from your well-pruned life? The sweet blessing will be not only your growth, but the sparks of new life in another soul.

And it will take your breath away.

When You Feel All Hope Is Gone

Our deeply personal story of pruning matters most to Jesus. Our compassionate, loving, self-sacrificing Savior walks every step with us. In fact, He carries us in His arms like a shepherd does His sheep.

I want to leave you with something I wrote toward the end of a recent season of pruning in my own life. I felt at times He had forgotten me. I wondered if He would, once again, be faithful to His Word. The storm raged on and the wounded place hurt until one day it didn't. This was my song of praise to Faithful and True:

"But then...with your hand you say, 'Peace be still.'

You see.

You move.

You give way to hope.

When it was all gone.

You say, 'For you, I did this.'

And the tears flow, and I am speechless.

This week, I have seen the spikes of that new growth beginning to push forth from the branch. I'm humbled by the thought. And excited to see how you will bring glory to this seemingly endless pruning of my heart.

Already, you have said and done so much to heal. I wonder how you decided it was to be now. In this now, secret prayers I have prayed with longing for years have begun to grow into your glorious yes.

One day soon, I'll be standing there in that full, yes.

And I will know without a shadow of a doubt that it was You. I wonder if the tears flow outwardly, or just in the place where that secret prayer once grew.

Either way, You will see. You will know. And we will sing grace."

And sing we did.

Traveling Mercies for Chapter 7:

Truth:

> "I have been crucified with Christ. It is no longer I who live, but Christ who lives in me. And the life I now live in the flesh I live by faith in the Son of God, who loved me and gave himself for me"
>
> *(Galatians 2:20, ESV)*

Think:

"The path of being OK with where you are often involves pruning, and pruning passes through the heart of the Gospel. Out of death, comes life. The death of Christ purchased my redemption, and I am called to be like Him."

Talk:

1. How has God used the two types of pruning in your life?

2. How have you changed since the beginning of your pruning journey?

3. Has God used your humbled position to speak powerfully to another person?

8 PERSEVERANCE

❧

Have you ever played the game Candy Land? If not, let me enlighten you. This board game of luck involves small people, who chase you down and wear you out until you sit and play it for hours. You are allowed to pick your gingerbread person marker (not the pink one) and draw cards that tell you where to move to on the board. The goal is to make it to the Candy Land castle while traveling up, up, up through the land of sweets. The problem is, along the way you may land on a space where you are taken back down to a spot you have already been to. Invariably, the four-year-old will never, ever fall down into the "forest of despair" involving super sticky taffy, but you will every time. She will win and you'll be stuck watching her happy dance. Of course, the small people will beg you to play again, so the whole process can start over. I suggest you mention some sort of adult chore (bummer) that absolutely needs to be finished right that very minute or your small people will continue to embarrass you again and again.

Many days, being OK with where you is a lot like being stuck inside a perpetual game of Candy Land. You may be moving along fine one day with the Candy Land castle in full sight. Only to find yourself going backward the very next day to a place you were last week. Like a silly children's game, you may need to repeat certain steps. Keep in mind, God is looking at your heart. He will respond to you in the most beautiful way even when you need do-overs along the way. Grace makes room for the days when we mess up, need a second chance, and have to find the will to persevere.

Enter Sarai Who Became Sarah

She was a wife who wanted to be a mama in the worst way. She walked beside her husband for years, even decades, before she lived the promise fulfilled. In between the promise made and the promise fulfilled she had her fair share of days when she was not ok with where she was. Her perseverance was far from perfect.

She took matters into her own hands:

> "And Sarai said to Abram, "Behold now,
> the Lord has prevented me from bearing
> children. Go into my servant; it may be that
> I shall obtain children by her."

(Genesis 16:2, ESV)

She blamed others when everything went as she had planned:

> "And he went in to Hagar, and she conceived. And when she saw that she had conceived, she looked with contempt on her mistress... Then Sarai dealt harshly with her, and she fled from her."
>
> *(Genesis 16:4,6,ESV)*

She laughed at the promise:

> "The Lord said to Abraham, 'Why did Sarah laugh and say, "Shall I indeed bear a child, now that I am old?" Is anything too hard for the Lord? At the appointed time I will return to you, and about this time next year, and Sarah will have a son.'"
>
> *(Genesis 18:13,14, ESV)*

As we have the chance to walk beside her through the years of waiting, we see so much of ourselves in her story. I know I have been her time and time again. I want things to go my way, so I push and pull until I manufacture my own artificial blessing. It ends up being less than perfect and I am found crying in my coffee wondering what I was thinking.

But God never wavers one bit off the mark of His own promise. He is faithful to His Word, every single time:

> "The LORD visited Sarah as he had said, and the LORD did to Sarah as he had promised. And Sarah conceived and bore Abraham a son in his old age at the time of which God had spoken to him. Abraham called the name of his son who was born to him, Isaac."

(Genesis 21:1-3, ESV)

She who laughed at the promise, found joy in it and named her son Isaac, which means "he laughs."

> "And Sarah said, 'God has made laughter for me; everyone who hears will laugh over me.'"

(Genesis 21:6, ESV)

Maybe with old age comes the ability to laugh at yourself, but I think Sarah and Abraham were bubbling over with joy here. They could see, touch, and hold the promise in their hands. Every time they called Isaac to come to dinner they would be reminded they had laughed at the promise God made—but God never once did.

Perseverance at times is not pretty. In the days that followed, Sarah still persevered imperfectly. She ran her servant off in a fit of jealousy and probably had to swallow a big dose of pride upon her return. She made a fine mess out of life in the tent of Abraham. Truthfully, I am really no better.

My mess has included gut-wrenching worry. I have let fear paralyze me at times. During the not OK days I've been guilty of jealousy and believing the lie that the Lord was holding out on me. I've held tightly to my own plans and stomped off in anger when I felt forgotten. My own perseverance has been stopped dead in its tracks because of my sin. I know better, to be sure. These things didn't move me through the hard days any quicker. But the sin of self has deep roots, and to remove it the Lord had to dig deeply into my heart. In the end, Sarah is a reminder that God's grace is a river that runs deeper and He can use our messes for His glory. For this, I am ever grateful.

What To Do on the Hard Days

My girls are dancers. My oldest has been taking ballet for eight years and last year she started dancing on pointe. The transition was painful. Every Monday I would pick her up from dance class and she would be in tears. We had many tough conversations about quitting and persevering. See, in order to dance on pointe, you have to deaden the nerves in your feet so they no longer tell you how painful the dance is. The hard days are filled with pain. She made the decision to push through the pain.

When her first recital came, I was mesmerized when

I saw her pull her one hundred and ten pound frame up on her toes. She was a vision of grace and beauty with the most pleasant smile on her face. She danced and I'm pretty sure I heard Leann Womack singing "I Hope You Dance" in my head.

What I want for my girls, and myself, is to learn on the hard days we dance anyway. We listen for the song of grace that is always playing somewhere and know what is being produced in and through us can't happen any other way.

> "Not only that, but we rejoice in our suffer-
> ings, knowing that suffering produces en-
> durance, and endurance produces character,
> and character produces hope, and hope does
> not put us to shame, because God's love has
> been poured into our hearts through the
> Holy Spirit who has been given to us."

(Romans 5:3-5, ESV)

If dancing were easy, everyone would be a prima bal-lerina. So few make it because the pain is too much for them to endure. Our spiritual lives are the same aren't they? When we suddenly find ourselves not OK with where we are, we have a choice to quit. But if we continue to walk with Christ through the process, He will bring us out on the other side with a deeper character only birthed through suffering and fertilized by enduring hope.

Gabby Douglas knows this full well. She was on the verge of quitting because the work it took to become a competitive Olympic gymnast was grueling. In fact, it almost sent her home instead of to London. When it was all said and done, with a gold medal or two around her neck this is what she said:

"It means so much, all the hard work and dedication and effort put in the gym and hard days," Douglas explained. "And hard days are the best because that's where champions are made, so if you push through the hard days you can get through anything." Gabby Douglas, Olympic Gold Medalist.[1]

Perseverance gives way to perspective in the end. She said, "The hard days are the best … This is where champions are made." Why do we resist the hard days? This is truly where God's spirit makes us into champions of faith. If we allow Him to, that is.

Baby Steps on the Bus

Perspective is hindsight of course and this does little to help us on the hard days. Of course it helps to find examples of those who have been there and are willing to tell us to keep moving forward.

"Now faith is the assurance of things hoped for, the convictions of things not seen. For by it the people of old received their commendation. By faith we understand that the universe was created by the word of God, so that what is seen was not made out of things that are visible."

(Hebrews 11:1-3, ESV)

Hebrews chapter eleven is often called the hall of faith because it goes on to list those people of old who received faith commendations. Guess who appears in this long list?

"By faith Sarah herself received power to conceive, even when she was past the age, since she considered him faithful who had promised."

(Hebrews 11:11, ESV)

This is the same imperfect Sarah who laughed at the promise, manipulated her own situation, and blamed others when she was not OK with where she was. In her small, mustard seed of faith, she considered Him faithful who had promised. And when she was beyond the age of becoming a mama, He made it so. Glory to God. He does amazing things when we place ourselves in His hands.

One of my all-time favorite quotable movies is "What About Bob." Bob is having a rough time making it through life and his counselor, played by Richard Dreyfuss, creates a method for him of taking small steps to move toward his larger life goals. The idea being if you can take many small steps, you will eventually arrive at your destination.

In one scene, Bob, (Bill Murray) is getting on a crowded

bus because he is desperate to see his counselor who has gone on vacation with his family. Bob is heard repeating to himself over and over, "Baby steps on the bus … baby steps to my seat … baby steps off the bus …" Finally, Bob perseveres and makes it to his doctor's door step, one baby step at a time.

To persevere and walk on with God, we need to realize we can take baby steps of faith, too. I love how Lysa Ter-keurst says it:

"Imperfect changes are slow steps of progress wrapped in grace … imperfect progress."[2]

Our perseverance can be slow, and many days it will be. Like Sarah we can keep moving on and on when we consider Him faithful and remember His promises. And, we can do it one baby step at a time.

Looking Back to Move Forward

Sometimes, we don't see how far we have come until we look back and see it in black and white. I have put my words in journals for years. Although now I write more publicly on my blog, I believe in the value of keeping a faith journal. I can't tell you how many times I've been dusting off shelves only to be distracted by a found four-year-old journal. Reading my heart on the page peels back the layers of doubt quickly. It is like sending an email to yourself in the future. I got this idea from Jon Acuff in his book *Quitter*. Either way it is powerful.

I want to encourage you to write down your thoughts and feelings and put them somewhere, starting today. Pour out your heart without thought of how many times you write the word "that" or caring what others may think. You will only be writing for two. The first reader being Jesus, and He knows what you mean however you write it. The second reader will be you, in a few weeks or years when you have the gift of hindsight. Maybe, just maybe, you will be in another difficult place and you will be able to see how God's faithfulness played out in your own life a few years before.

I think this truth is best displayed in the pages of God's Word. As we read it and see how God moved throughout the ages, in the lives of people just like you and me, we gain a third-person perspective.

> "For whatever was written in former
> days was written for our instruction, that
> through endurance and through the en-
> couragement of the Scriptures we might
> have hope."

(Romans 15:4, ESV)

We learn from watching them. We see His hand upon them and our hearts gain strength from their testimonies. It stirs up the hope within us to believe He will do the same for us.

Perseverance grows from time well spent in the Word. Especially on the days when we can't see how in the world

God is going to work out our own journeys. We need His Word to guide us and give us hope while pouring out our own on the page. And we need to do it one baby step at a time. Like Sarah, in the end, we will find Him faithful.

Traveling Mercies for Chapter 8:

Truth:

> "Not only that, but we rejoice in our sufferings, knowing that suffering produces endurance, and endurance produces character, and character produces hope, and hope does not put us to shame, because God's love has been poured into our hearts through the Holy Spirit who has been given to us."

(Romans 5:3-5, ESV)

Think:

"When we suddenly find ourselves not OK with where we are, we have a choice to quit. But if we continue to walk with Christ through the process, He will bring us out on the other side with a deeper character only birthed through suffering and fertilized by enduring hope."

Talk:

1. How has your perseverance been imperfect at times?

2. Does the fact that Sarah made it into the "Hall of Faith" inspire you?

3. Why do we resist the hard days where God is making us into spiritual champions?

9 LIVE THANKFUL

❧

"I wonder, Lord, how do I honor You, while I am still desiring the very thing You saw fit to cut away?"

And then as soon as I take the next breath, I have my answer.

He whispers ... "Give thanks."

Life has a tendency to go on and on. When you are not OK with where you are, you still have to get up, make the coffee, go to work, and feed the kids. There is some comfort in the routine, I confess. Other days, I'm so busy surviving my life I forget this is my life. You only get one time around, right? It needs to be lived, counted, remembered, and celebrated. Each moment is precious. This moment is precious. A few years ago God invited me to open my eyes to the wonder around me. Even when I was not particularly OK with where I was sitting.

With a Single Word, God Called Me Out

My pastor challenges our congregation every January to find a word to frame our year. He asks us in December to pray and seek God's heart on the matter. Almost without exception, God has answered my prayers and strongly spoken a word to me. In 2010, the word He gave me was thankfulness.

The timing was key. My fourth daughter was born in the fall of 2009 and a sweet gift for sure. However sweet, she was not a fan of sleeping. In fact, she did not sleep much the first two and half years of her life. You could say, and I certainly would, that I was not OK. I was tired and at the end of my rope.

So with a single word, God called me out. He challenged me to begin where I was and start counting gifts. He said I could not look on down the road, when sleep may come in shifts of five-six hours at a time. He wanted me to start counting now. The date was January 11. Early in the morning I had read this:

"When you bring Me prayer requests, lay out your concerns before me. Speak to Me candidly; pour out your heart. *Then thank me for the answers that I have set into motion long before you can discern results.* When your requests come to mind again, continue to thank Me for the answers that are on the way. If you keep on stating your concerns to Me, you will live in a state of tension. When you thank Me for how I am answering your prayers, your mind-set becomes much more positive. Thankful prayers keep your focus on My Presence and My Promises." Sarah Young, *Jesus Calling* for January 11 (emphasis mine).

The next day, January 12, 2010, began with a flurry of activity at our house. I was packing my ten-year-old daughter for her first mission trip. She and her dad were headed to Haiti with an organization near to our hearts called New Missions. They were part of a team of twenty or so dads and kids going to pass out shoe box gifts to hundreds of Haitian children. My daughter was going to give a gift to our newly sponsored "daughter" named Shelcie. We were excited, busy, and nervous. But mostly, we were grateful to have the opportunity to introduce our oldest daughter to a compassion-filled ministry to children and families in need.

The phone rang while we were trying to cram everything into her suitcase. My friend Krystal, whose husband works for New Missions, called to tell me there was an earthquake in Haiti and she thought the trip might be cancelled. A few minutes later, her intuition was confirmed when the leader of our trip called to say the trip was off. As we turned on the television to watch the news reports, my heart was overwhelmed. The images coming out of Port Au Prince were devastating. The destruction from the 7.0 earthquake was too much for my mind to comprehend.

If the earthquake had occurred a mere twelve hours later, my husband and daughter would have been in the middle of it. I thought back to the sentence from *Jesus Calling* the day before, "thank me for answers I have set into motion long before you can discern the results." I had not thought to ask God to protect them from an earthquake. But God had already set the plan in motion.

I have no idea why God spared my family from this catastrophic event. I can tell you the mission they were headed to experienced some damage but no loss of life. I can also tell you long into the night after the first earthquake the Haitian people were heard singing and praising God for all He had done to protect them. They were heard singing. Can you imagine?

Thankfulness broke into my life in a profound way. I needed it, too. Weariness had become a habit of my heart. I desperately needed to change this destructive way of living. Gratitude became the key that unlocked the prison of discontent and set me free.

So, in 2010 I began being intentionally grateful for God's poured out blessings. I joined author of *One Thousand Gifts*, Ann Voskamp, and other gratitude-chasers on the same journey. Some days I counted gifts like coffee, date nights, and handmade cards . OK, I counted coffee more than once. I happen to be very grateful for coffee. Other days I counted gifts like safe travel for my husband, babies being born, and the strength to get through fourth grade math. I began to see the size of the gift really didn't matter, only that it was counted.

"It's the joy of the small that can make life large, and all wonder and worship can only grow out of small and humble things, " Ann Voskamp, *One Thousand Gifts*.[1]

My worship began to grow out of this small beginning of simply saying thank you to the One who is the giver of all good things:

> "Every good gift and every perfect gift is
> from above, coming down from the Father
> of lights with whom there is no variation or
> shadow due to change."

(James 1:7)

He gave. I counted. But it was not all sunshine and roses. Many days, thankfulness was hard. I found the words of Nancy Leigh DeMoss to be true:

"Gratitude is a lot more than jonquils and journaling pages. Gratitude is a lifestyle. A hard-fought, grace-infused biblical lifestyle." [2]

No, this was not a year of fluff. I learned a life lesson: thankfulness is a position of the heart. When I am thankful to God, my heart is turned toward His. When my heart is turned toward Him, I am able to see things with His perspective. The year of thankfulness was training my eyes to see, period.

Hidden Treasures and Counting Backwards

My husband's love language involves blackberry pie. I've been working for years to find the perfect combination of sweet and tart served on a crust that melts in our mouths. Oh, he would eat anything, but I have always wanted his eyes to sort of roll back into his head when he takes a bite and declares my blackberry pie State Fair worthy. I think I have finally found THE recipe which is really a combination of two. I use "Gayle's Pie Crust" and a filling I found online. The only problem is, I have to settle for frozen store bought berries. For years, this bothered me and seemed like defeat from the beginning. Let me tell you why.

When I was a little girl, my grandpa loved to go berry picking. We lived in the country and he would come out every summer in his overalls, sporting at least two berry buckets. Usually, my brother would accompany him on these nature hikes. Sometimes, I was asked to tag along. I would dutifully go, but I can tell you right here and now I did not like it much.

First of all, it was always the hottest day in July when the berries were ripe. Second of all, my hands would turn bluish-purple and hurt from the thorns I always seemed to find while picking. Plus, my grandpa was a quiet man and not much for conversation. I would chatter on and on and he would just say, "Mmmhuh ... Is that right?" I don't think he was really listening, now that I think of it.

Still, we would bring in a haul of beautiful Indiana wild blackberries for my mom and grandma to turn into the best jam you have ever tasted. Of course, there was also pie. I liked that part at least.

So, now, thirty-some years later, here I am with frozen,

store-bought berries in my pie. Frozen berries are tarter than wild berries. You have to work with the recipe to achieve the right taste. This is probably why it took me twenty years.

Do you know what counting gifts has done to my whiny, blackberry-picking heart?

- I am grateful I can find frozen blackberries.

- I am grateful for my husband who eats whatever blackberry surprise I sit in front of him.

- I am grateful for silly girls who insist on helping.

- I count on and on.

- I also count backwards for those hot July days when I got to go berry picking with my grandpa.

- I long for one more day with this simple man who taught me how to live quiet (or at least tried) and gave me the chance to slow down life.

These are the hidden treasures a year of thankfulness taught me to count, forward and backwards:

"I will give you hidden treasures,

riches stored in secret places,

so that you may know that I am the
LORD,

the God of Israel, who summons you by
name."

(Isaiah 45:3, NIV)

It took counting gifts day after day for months to simply
to train my eyes to see it. To see store-bought berries
can be pure joy, too. Big things or small, if we don't have
eyes to see them, they just slip away into the busyness of
our days and simply become the mundane. But counting
brings them out into the wide world of joy. And it takes us
right along with it.

We Take the Good, We Take the Bad

Yesterday, I sat and watched as my girls played red light
green light in a field and my husband snapped pictures.
I took the moment and framed it in my mind, silently
counting it. I smiled and realized after weeks of *counting
gifts* the treasure I take away is *the journey*.

There was a time, when I labeled only good things as
gifts. Sunrises are good, but cancer is bad. Girls who laugh
with their sisters are good, but being up all night with a
fussy baby is bad. So count the sunrises and happy girls as
gifts, but definitely not the cancer or the fussy baby. The
journey has taught me each one is to be counted because it

is a new way to rediscover who He is.

In the good, He just flat out overwhelms me with grace. Some days I see it coming for miles. Other days, I'm surprised by grace and the joy it brings with it. This reminds me of a series of images my husband took of my girls while we are at Sea World a couple of years ago. They were standing on a bridge watching a boat ride plummet down a steep hill. Two of my girls were watching the boat and one of my girls was standing nearby posing for her dad. The boat came down bringing a tidal wave with it. In the first frame the two girls who were focused on the dive responded accordingly. They tried to shelter themselves from the water and were screaming with joy. They were knowingly overwhelmed by it all.

My other daughter, the whole time eyes fixed on the camera, became part of the wave as well. Only, she was caught off-guard. Because my husband is a master photographer, he was able to shoot several pictures in a matter of seconds. Her sisters behind her fleeing, she was smiling innocently. The final frame found her a sopping wet mess. All were laughing and all together drenched.

His all-consuming gifts overwhelm like that day on the bridge—completely. We are taken in by His goodness whether we see it coming or not. Sometimes, like my daughter, we are caught unaware. Either way, His grace pours out on us wave after wave. And with it comes pure joy.

When I face the hard days He still overwhelms me

with grace. Take for example the day I found out my dad had cancer for the first time. I would not call that a good day or the phone call with my mom easy. But, sitting on my kitchen floor with tears streaming down my face, His goodness was ever present with me.

> "Even though I walk through the valley of
> the shadow of death, I will fear no evil,
> for you are with me;
> your rod and your staff, they comfort me."

(Psalm 23:4)

His comfort was a gift. His tender ministry to my mom that day, when neither my brother nor I could be with her, was a gift. The friends He sent to love on both my parents were all beautiful grace gifts. So too, was the way my dad's faith grew during the fight for his life. Cancer is not something any of us want knocking at our doors, but with it, God brings gifts which, if we have eyes to see, are overwhelmingly good. Either way, as Ann Voskamp so beautifully says, "All is grace." And because of that, everything He brings into my life is a gift and it is good.

What We Really Want When We Are Not OK

When my daughter Emma was about two years old, she would say, "I want something that I want." We would laugh and ask her what it was she wanted, and it was always something she perceived would make her life better.

At her age, this was usually a toy or a fancy ice cream dessert.

When we are not OK with where we are, we want something that we want, too. Our grown-up wants look more sophisticated and maybe even seem like good things. We want security. We want life to be easy, don't we? We ask, and sometimes He gives us these things. But sometimes He says no. C.S. Lewis says:

> "The security we crave would teach us to rest our hearts in this world and oppose an obstacle to our return to God: a few moments of happy love, a landscape, a symphony, a merry meeting with our friends, a bathe or a football match, have no such tendency. Our Father refreshes us on the journey with some pleasant inns, but will not encourage us to mistake them for home."[3]

I'm so grateful our Father refreshes us on the journey. We need it for sure. But, the bottom line is, this is not our home. When we find ourselves in place of longing for what we wish we had, we need to see this as a cue to turn our hearts and eyes toward the eternal.

My friend Angie shared something with me recently her pastor once said:

"This side of heaven, life is really only about a four on a scale of one to ten. I expect life to be a ten all the time! But it's just not … we have to stop and cherish the moments when we are pushing a five or six and long for heaven even more!"[4]

Does not being OK with where you are create in you a longing for heaven? Oh friend, this needs to be our prayer. Can we give thanks for all things because when He says no, it makes our hearts want heaven more? Because, I think, when it really it comes down to it, that is what we really want anyway.

The Victory Lap

I counted gifts daily in 2010 and on into 2011. I hit 1,000 around summer time when we were standing on a beautiful mountain in Colorado. It seemed perfect actually, because the climb to the top had not been so easy. The view however, was spectacular. We took a picture, all six of us together and I wrote about it later. Only, I didn't feel finished. So, in 2012 I started counting 1,000 gifts again. I took a victory lap, like all good fifth-year college seniors do. This time, by focusing on three gifts per day, I finished easily by Christmas.

Years ago, God shed light on a verse from a tiny book in the Old Testament called Habakkuk. The verse says:

> "Though the fig tree should not blossom,
> nor fruit be on the vines, the produce of the
> olive will fail and the fields yield no food,
> the flock be cut off from the fold and there

be no herd in the stalls, yet I will rejoice in
the LORD; I will take joy in the God of
my salvation."

(Habakkuk 3:17,18)

I know the place of longing, pruning, and letting go
of dreams can seem like a lifeless wasteland. But living
thankful has shown me we can not only shift our own
perspectives, but we can be a bold witness for Christ in the
midst of it:

*"A grateful man or woman will be a breath of fresh air in
a world contaminated by bitterness and discontentment.* And
the person whose gratitude is a byproduct of and a re-
sponse to the redeeming grace of God will showcase the
heart of the gospel in a way that is winsome and compelling." Nancy Leigh DeMoss, *Choosing Gratitude*, p 24
(emphasis mine).

I want to be a woman who is a breath of fresh air,
winsome and compelling. I want to stand with the Ha-
bakkuks of the world and say, "I will rejoice, no matter
what my eyes may see in front of me." I want to point to
the redeeming grace of God in my life and if it is the only
reason I have to give thanks, then I will do it with all of
my heart. Join me?

Traveling Mercies for Chapter 9:

Truth:

> "Though the fig tree should not blossom,
> nor fruit be on the vines, the produce of the
> olive will fail and the fields yield no food,
> the flock be cut off from the fold and there
> be no herd in the stalls, yet I will rejoice in
> the LORD; I will take joy in the God of
> my salvation."

(Habakkuk 3:17,18)

Think:

"No, this was not a year of fluff. I learned a life lesson: thankfulness is a position of the heart. When I am thankful to God, my heart is turned toward His. When my heart is turned toward Him, I am able to see things with His perspective. The year of thankfulness was training my eyes to see, period."

Talk:

1. What are some hidden treasures God has provided for you recently?

2. Does not Being OK with Where You Are create a longing for heaven in your heart?

3. How would living thankful change your life right now?

10 WORSHIP ANYWAY

⟨❦⟩

I have this theory. When we are not OK with where we are, we feel it so deep down in our bones it colors everything we do. Sometimes, we live in this place for so long we don't see our passion for life is gone. We set up shop in a place called Pity Party, loving our own misery a little too much. We kind of like our safe, sad place. But the Lord wants so much more for us. He loves us too much to leave us there. Author C.S. Lewis writes:

> "It would seem that our Lord finds our
> desires not too strong, but too weak. We are
> half-hearted creatures, fooling about with
> drink and sex and ambition when infinite
> joy is offered us, like an ignorant child who
> wants to go on making mud pies in a slum
> because he cannot imagine what is meant
> by the offer of a holiday at the sea. We are
> far too easily pleased."[1]

Have you been making mud pies lately, too? Are you fooling around with all the wrong things to try and make it all better? For me, those wrong things look more like shopping or a bag of M&M's, preferably at the same time. Still, I sit in the slum willingly, crafting my own perfect mud pie, and watch the cruise ship of infinite joy go by. I can't imagine I have a ticket to ride. But I do. And it has one word stamped on it: worship.

"Without worship we go about miserable; that's why we have all the troubles we have." A. W. Tozer[2]

I think Tozer is spot on. We are miserable because in our discontentment we have lost our desire to worship. We feel forgotten and our souls are cast downward. We have believed the lie worship is reserved for all those other girls who are loving life and telling everyone about it. The problem with this line of thinking is we make worship about how we are feeling, and quite frankly that is not at all what worship is about.

> "Eternal One, my True God, I cried out to You for help; You mended the shattered pieces of my life."
>
> *(Psalm 30:2, The Voice)*

These are words penned by David. They tell my story, too. He was not a mom like me. He was a king. He was not being overwhelmed by toddlers or arguing with a teenager. He was running for His life from a crazy man, which may sort of be the same thing. He was living a shattered pieced together life and in the midst of it, he cried out to God for help.

David was plucked from a simple life as a sheep herder and anointed king. He waited years for this promise to come to fruition. In the middle he was hunted like an animal by Saul. I think it is safe to say he spent a fair amount of time not being OK with where he was in life. I love his honesty. I love his willingness to live life unveiled in front of God and others. Mostly, I love his heart. God said it was like His own. Time and time again, David saw his hope was in God. I love this quote from Beth Moore about him:

"When other hearts were *prone* to wander, David's heart was *prone* to worship." (emphasis mine)[3]

The word prone has a couple of different meanings. The first is:

prone: "inclined"[4]

Another definition includes:

prone: "A body position in which one lies flat with the chest down and back up"[5].

I love this play on words. It is rich with meaning. David's heart was *inclined* to worship. In other words, his heart was bent toward an attitude of worship all the time. The second type of prone is often seen as the physical act of worship. I'm guessing David was found face-planted on the ground more than once by those who knew him well.

David was not too proud to go face down before the Lord. He worshipped with all that he was.

David had every right to complain. He had every reason to blame his situation on others. But he didn't. He chose to worship on the days when he probably would rather not. I think there are three key things we can learn from David about worship during the times we are not OK with where we are.

Determine to praise God through every situation.

> "I will praise the Eternal in every moment *through every situation*. Whenever I speak, my words will always praise Him."
>
> *(Psalm 34:1, The Voice)*

If David had written one verse or one Psalm like this, I think we would be moved. But this theme is repeated in some form throughout all of his writings. David often strikes the same cord. He determines to praise God at all times.

He worshiped when:

Guarding the sheep.

Fighting off lions.

Killing a giant.

Running from Saul.

It didn't matter what David was doing or how life came at him. He decided beforehand he would praise God no matter what.

I wonder what it would look like in my life if I determined everyday to praise God, regardless. I think it would show up loud and clear to the people around me. It reminds me of a sweet woman I met this week in the bathroom at the Charlotte airport. I rushed in after getting off the plane, along with several others. The woman I met was overflowing with praise and joy. She said hello to everyone who walked in. She shouted, "*God bless you*" and "*You are beautiful.*" Every woman who stood at the mirror heard her singing. Her outlook was contagious. Each women who exited the restroom said goodbye to her and they smiled. Who was she? She was working in the restroom. Washing sinks, cleaning the facilities and mopping floors was her job. She also took care to place mints in a basket and cups of Listerine for the ladies who dropped in. This woman was determined to be joyful and I'm just guessing she was also a woman who was prone to worship. Could you praise Jesus while working in a public restroom? What a blessing she was to me. I want to be a blessing like that in the lives of others, too.

Give Testimony

"When I needed the Lord, I looked for Him; I called out to Him, and He heard me and responded. He came and rescued me from everything that made me so afraid."

(Psalm 34:4)

David liked to testify. He wanted everyone to know what God in heaven had done for him each and every day. "I needed Him. I called out to Him—and He answered!" I think David was one of those people who was always telling his story. He talked to anyone who would listen. He was in the business of telling all the good things God had done for him. It brought him joy to do so.

When I was a little girl, my little Baptist church held Sunday night services right after youth group. The mood was more casual than the morning service time, and most nights the pastor would say, *"Does anyone have a testimony they'd like to share?"* Usually, a man name Bill would tell how God had been faithful and everyone would nod their heads and say, "Amen." Then, Lois Ann would play the "Count Your Blessings" on the piano like nobody had ever played it before and we'd all sing along.

Maybe David knew testifying was not just so others could hear how God had been faithful, but so he could hear it, too. Naming blessings one by one is a great way to remember. A heart prone to worship needs to remember all God has done.

Take others with you.

> "Taste of His goodness; see how wonder-
> ful the Eternal truly is. Anyone who puts
> trust in Him will be blessed and comforted.
> Revere the Eternal, you His saints, for those
> who worship Him will possess everything
> important in life."

(Psalm 34:8,9, The Voice)

David was gifted by God to lead people well. Leading seemed to come naturally to him. But David was not only interested in leading armies or city officials. He was committed to leading people to the heart of God. He exhorts them, "Taste His goodness. See how wonderful He is." He led people to experience God in their everyday lives and he inspired them to worship.

If David had been a priest I think this would be understandable. But David was not sitting in church on a soft-padded pews. He was hiding in caves, fighting battles, and sitting around campfires with hungry men. He was doing all he could do to stay alive and trusting in God almighty to fulfill His promises to Him. In the middle of it all, not only did his heart worship, he desired to lead others to do the same. He had a powerful position of influence, and he chose to take others into the throne room of God.

We all know David was not perfect. I certainly don't want to put him on a pedestal of praise. But Psalm after Psalm, and verse after verse, shows a man who knew even if he was not OK with where his life was at the moment, God was still to be worshiped. Because He was worthy of it.

When I've Tried to Edit Worship

A few years ago I was let go from a ministry I dearly loved. The story behind the reason is not so important. The bottom line was, a few changes were made and I was no longer needed to serve in the way I had come to love. I wasn't given a choice, I was simply asked to step aside. I will tell you right now, I was devastated and my worship of God suffered.

I remember sitting in church and my heart physically hurting. I longed to serve God in this way. I wrestled. I fussed to my husband. I whined to God many, many, many times. He knew exactly how I felt.

He said, "Worship anyway."

Worship anyway? Really?

I was not sure how to do this. So I made my mud pies, licked my wounds and sat in the slum of my own hurt heart. You could say I pouted. My mom would say I crafted this art by age ten. Now, in my thirties I was a professional.

What did my heavenly Father do while I was sitting cross-armed and crying? He wooed me. He drew me. He called me to Himself without one bit of condemnation.

He did so through my years of gratitude chasing. He even used a year-long study on grace to remind me He wanted my heart and not my act of service. He called me upward and finally it all came apart one day when I went to the altar to lay it all down before Him. The song my friend Christie was singing at the time was called "You Covered Me."[6] It spoke to my heart, and turned me toward Jesus.

Suddenly, I realized even when I was not OK with where I was, I was covered. All He went through for me on the cross covered my broken places. I could live through it with a worshipful heart because of who He was, not where I sat. Grace and love all mixed up together poured out over me that day, and for the first time in a long time I let my heart receive it. I tried to edit worship from my life because it hurt too much. In reality, it was the one thing I needed most.

The Call to Worship Anyway

Do you remember chapter one and the story of Jonah? Our look at his deep-sea fishing trip was mainly about him finally admitting he was not OK with where he was. I also mentioned this:

> "While he was admitting his not 'OKness'
> he also did something else very important.

He remembered all that was right about
God."

And then, Jonah's prayer from inside the
fish turned into a worship session.

"But I will offer sacrifices to you with songs
of praise,
and I will fulfill all my vows.
For my salvation comes from the Lord
alone."

(Jonah 2:9)

Worship is all about remembering what is good and
right about God and telling Him about it. This is exactly
what he did. He took his eyes off of himself and placed
them on our Lord, God almighty. With God in full view,
"the things of life grow strangely dim."[7] And what Jonah
saw was glory—His. Even though Jonah was literally on
the verge of death inside a fish, he worshipped anyway.

Jonah's song of praise is a beautiful picture of this verse
written by David:

"Oh magnify the Lord with me, let us exalt
His name together."

(Psalm 34:3, NASB)

The call to worship anyway is to magnify the Lord,

like Jonah. Of course, we can't make God bigger than He already is. A.W. Tozer said:

"Most of us see God too small; our God is too little. David said, "O magnify the Lord with me," and "magnify" doesn't mean to make God big. You can't make God big. But you can see Him big." *The Missing Jewel,* p. 21

- When we worship anyway, it grows our view of God, and shrinks our troubles.

- When we worship anyway, it lifts us higher, but also brings us lower in reverence. When we worship anyway, we have the chance to be like David and bring others along with us.

- When we worship anyway, we understand the real reason we are here is to glorify Him no matter what is going on in our lives

Will you magnify the Lord with me, sweet friend? Will you join me in singing this song?

"Sing, all you who remain faithful! *Pour out your hearts* to the Eternal with praise and melodies; let grateful music *fill the air and* bless His name.

His wrath, you see, is fleeting, but His grace lasts a lifetime. The deepest pains may linger through the night, but joy greets the soul with the *smile of* morning."

(Psalm 30:4-5, The Voice Translation)

I know you may not totally be OK with where you are. You aren't required to be to worship. You may feel like the night is going to last forever, but I promise the joy of the morning is coming for you. His grace is going to outlive your life. And on the days when you wish you could trade yours for another, go ahead and pour out your heart. Dear girl, He hears it as a praise song. Do you believe it?

The thing about worship is it moves us and transforms us. It may well be the key to seeing everything in our life as stepping stones to getting us right where He wants us:

Hearts open.

Eyes on Him.

Hands to heaven.

Ready and willing to do His will.

We worship.

And the dawn rises with the sun while our soul sings joy. Morning has come.

Traveling Mercies from Chapter 10:

Truth:

> "I will praise the Eternal in every moment
> through every situation. Whenever I speak,
> my words will always praise Him."
>
> ***(Psalm 34:1, The Voice)***

Think:

"Suddenly, I realized even when I was not OK with where I was, I was covered. All He went through for me on the cross covered my broken places. I could live through it with a worshipful heart because of who He was, not where I sat."

Talk:

1. Be honest. Have you been making mud pies lately?

2. How does David's heart for worship minister to you?

3. Can you commit right now, no matter where you are on your journey, to "Worship Anyway"?

Afterword

Take the Next Step

I graduated from high school in 1989 when big hair was cool, Michael was the king of pop, and Indiana Jones was our hero. Do you remember how we waited with anticipation for "The Last Crusade?" We were still on the edge of our seats when, towards the end of the movie, Indy was forced to take a leap of faith.

Standing at the precipice, Indiana was faced with a decision. His mission required him to make it to the other side. There was no other way. Would he keep going? Would he turn back? Would he take the next step? What would Indy do?

With his heart pounding he reminded himself of the words, "leap of faith." He breathed heavy, lifted his foot high, and by faith placed it down on thin air. But when his foot fell, it was touching solid ground! Suddenly the *leap* of faith turned into a *bridge* of faith. His human eyes could not see it because this bridge was made for eyes that see through faith to the other side.

> "The path we walk is charted by faith, not by what we see with our eyes."
>
> *(2 Corinthians 5:7, The Voice)*

Sweet friend, the thing I want to leave you with is this: the path you are walking now is best seen with eyes of faith. The next step you take may feel like stepping into thin air. But as you stand here, you must remember that God has gone before you and installed a bridge of faith.

He has gone before.

He walks beside.

You can take the next step.

I love this encouragement from Amy Carmichael, "If only the next step is clear, then the one thing to do is take it! Don't pledge your Lord or yourself to any steps beyond what you know. You don't see them yet." *You Are My Hiding Place, p.25*

Your next step of faith may be to finally admit you are not OK. It may be to begin living thankful and counting your blessings. Maybe you need to call a friend and meet for coffee or spend some time in worship. I'm guessing, right now, in the quiet of your heart you know what step I'm talking about.

This is the promise I want to leave with you:

> "And He will be leading you. He'll be with you, and He'll never fail you or abandon you. So don't be afraid."

> *Deuteronomy 31:8 (The Voice)*

The confidence we have in taking the next step is this: we do not walk alone. Not ever.

Looking Forward,

Stacey

REFERENCES

Chapter 1: Admit It

1. A.W. Tozer, *The Pursuit of God* (Camp Hill, PA, Christian Publications, Inc.,1993),30.

Chapter 2: Let It Go

1. Merriam-Websters online, s.v. "surrender," accessed August 17, 2013, http://www.merriam-webster.com/dictionary/surrender.

2. C.S. Lewis, *Mere Christianity* (HaperOne, 2001), 202-203.

Chapter 3: Removing the Veil of Fine

1. Emily P. Freeman, *Graceful: Letting Go of the Try Hard Life* (Grand Rapids, MI, Revell, 2012), 19.

2. Brooke McGlothlin and Stacey Thacker, *Hope for the Weary Mom: Where God Meets You in Your Mess* (Lexington, KY, Create Space, 2012), 22.

3. Brooke McGlothlin and Stacey Thacker, *Hope for*

the Weary Mom: Where God Meets You in Your Mess (Lexington, KY, Create Space, 2012), 22.

4. Jamerrill Stewart, November 18, 20011,review of *Hope for the Weary Mom*, (blog) http://www.hope-forthewearymom.com/testimonies/.

Chapter 5: Standing on the Promises

1. To learn more about reading the *Bible in Ninety Days,* go to http://biblein90days.org/.

2. *Amy Carmichael, You Are My Hiding Place: A 40 Day Journey in the Company of Amy Carmichael,* by David Hazzard. (Bloomington, MN, Bethany House Publishers, 1991), 50.

3. Webster's Dictionary of 1828, s.v. "stand," accessed August 17,2013, http://1828.mshaffer.com/d/word/stand.

Chapter 6: You May Need a Cheerleader

1. Corrie Ten Boom, *You Are My Hiding Place* (Germany, Chosen Books, 1971), 217.

2. *Finding Nemo*. Dir. Andrew Stanton and Lee Unkrich. Walt Disney Pictures, Pixar Animation Studios. 2003. Film.

Chapter 7: On Pruning

1. Michael Rosen, *We're Going on a Bear Hunt* (New York, Little Simon,1989).

2. Webster's Dictionary of 1828, s.v. "prune" accessed August 15, 2013, http://1828.mshaffer.com/d/search/word,prune.

3. Wikipedia, s.v. "Pruning", accessed August 15, 2013, http://en.wikipedia.org/wiki/Pruning; August 15, 2013.

4. A. W. Tozer, *The Pursuit of God*, (Camp Hill, PA, Christian Publications, Inc.,1993), 44.

5. Elisabeth Elliot, *Keep A Quiet Heart*, (Ann Arbor, MI, Servant Publications, 1995), 41.

6. Ginny Owens, "If You Want Me To", (blog) http://ginnyowensmusic.com/if-you-want-me-to-the-best-of-ginny-owens/.

Chapter 8: Persevere

1. Elaine Quijano, "Olympic champion Gabby Douglas a hometown hero to aspiring gymnasts," CBS News, August 12, 2013, http://www.cbsnews.com/8301-18563_162-57486697/olympic-champion-gabby-douglas-a-hometown-hero-to-aspiring-g

2. Lysa Terkeurst, *Unglued*, (Grand Rapids, MI, Zondervan, 2012), 14.

Chapter 9: Live Thankful

1. Ann Voskamp, *One Thousand Gifts*, (Grand Rapid, MI, Zondervan 2011).

2. Nancy Leigh DeMoss, *Choosing Gratitude*, (Chicago, IL, Moody Publishers, 2009), 29.

3. C.S. Lewis, *The C.S. Lewis Bible*, (New York, Harper Collins, 2010), 1212.

4. From comments on Stacey Thacker, "How to be OK with Where You Are Chapter 5", 29 Lincoln Avenue(blog), June 24, 2013, http://www.29lincolnave-nue.com/2013/06/how-to-be-ok-with-where-you-are-chapter-5 .

Chapter 10: Worship Anyway

1. C. S. Lewis, *The Weight of Glory, and Other Addresses,* (New York, Harper One, 2001), http://www.go-odreads.com/work/quotes/1629232-the-weight-of-glory.

2. A.W. Tozer, *The Missing Jewel*, (8-9). Excerpt from *Tozer on Christian Leadership*, June 8, (Camp Hill,

3. PA, Wing Spread Publishers, 2001) compiled by Ron Eggert.

4. Beth Moore, *David: Seeking a Heart Like His:* (Lifeway Press, Nashville,TN, 2010), 131.

5. Merriam Webster Online, s.v. "prone", accessed August 16, 2013, http://www.merriam-webster.com/dictionary/prone.

6. Wikipedia, s.v. "prone", accessed August 16, 2013, http://en.wikipedia.org/wiki/Prone.

7. Doug Pierce, "You Covered Me", McKinney Music (adm. Lifeway Music), 1999.

8. Hellen H. Lemmel, "Turn Your Eyes Upon Jesus", 1922, http://www.hymnlyrics.org/mostpopular-hymns/turn_your_eyes_upon_jesus.php

Free Resources

Scripture Cards:

To print and share based on Chapter 5 "Standing on the Promises."

The "OK" Covenant:

- I can be OK because I have a promise to stand on.

- I can be OK because because life is full of awe inspiring gifts.

- I can be OK because I can worship God anyway.

- I can be OK because God has covered all my broken places with grace.

- I can be OK not because of where I sit, but because of who God is.

Available in a Pinterst Ready Pin or as a free download.

These resources can be found on my website here or go to: http://www.29lincolnavenue.com/being-ok-with-where-you-are-freebies/

WITH HEARTFELT THANKS

Mike: You were the first person to call me a writer and give me the platform to work out my words. Thank you for believing in my gift before I was able to. I am grateful for all you have done to make this little book possible. We make a great team. Always.

Emma, Abby, Caroline and Alison: You are the best part of it all. Thank you for making me a mommy and giving me time each day to write in my favorite corner. I can't wait to see what God has in store for you. I love being on the front row cheering for you! I love you so much!

Those who read rough words: (Angie, Brooke, Sara, Krystal, Gretchen, Crystal, Lara, Marissa, Teri Lynne, Tanya, Kaitlyn, Karin) Thank you for persevering to the end and encouraging me in the midst of the hard days. I am beyond thankful for your time and support!

Launch Team: You helped launch a dream! I can't thank you enough for sending this out into the big wide world!

Friends of 29 Lincoln Avenue Blog: I asked you to show up on Mondays to help me write *Being OK with Where You Are* and you actually came. I wish I could buy you all coffee and cheesecake. You deserve it! Thank you!

Sandra: You edit words and God smiles. Thank you friend.

Robin: You have walked with me every step of my journey. I'm so glad I crashed your Bible Study 24 years ago.

Lisa: I could not ask for a better *Modern Day Ruth*. Thank you for casting vision when I could not see and leading me to God's Word when I needed it most.

12 Women Who I Once Shared a Table with for 3 years: The Tozer quotes are for you. Love you. Miss you.

Jesus: I will worship at your feet today, tomorrow, and for eternity.

ABOUT THE AUTHOR

Stacey Thacker is Mike's wife and the mother of four vibrant girls. She is a believer and writer who loves God's Word and connecting with women. You can find her blogging at 29LincolnAvenue.com where she seeks to encourage your heart, grow in faith, and talk about the stuff of life. She is also the owner of MothersofDaughters.com a monthly e-zine for moms. Stacey is the co-author of Hope for the Weary Mom: Where God Meets you in Your Mess. You can find her on Facebook or on Twitter, where she usually hangs out with a cup of coffee in her hand.

Other Books By Stacey Thacker:

What God Wants You to Know: A 31 Day Devotional

Praying for Our Daughters: (A Mothers of Daughters Resource)

Hope for the Weary Mom: Where God Meets You in Your Mess – Co-authored with Brooke McGlothlin.

Author's Websites:

29 Lincoln Avenue:

http://29lincolnavenue.com

Mothers of Daughters:

http://mothersofdaugthers.com

Hope for the Weary Mom:

http://hopeforthewearymom.com

Twitter:

http://twitter.com/stacey29lincoln

Facebook:

https://www.facebook.com/29lincolnavenue

ALSO FROM STACEY

What God Wants You To Know: A 31 Day Journey (Sampler)

(Days 1-5)

Day 1

"How God thinks of us is not only more important, but infinitely more important" (C.S. Lewis). Years of Christian discipleship, Bible study, churchgoing had been about me thinking *about* God; practicing eucharisteo {thanksgiving} was the very first I had really considered at length what God *thought of me* — this ridiculous and relentlessly pursuing love, so bold. Everywhere, everything, Love! — Ann Voskamp, *One Thousand Gifts*, page 205

Are you tired of doing? Do you think you need to impress God? Have you ever felt small and insignificant? What would it feel like to let God paint His promises across your heart?

God's heart for you is bigger than anything you can imagine. In fact, we are only going to slip our tiny little toes into the sea of all He wants you to know during the next 30 days.

My prayer for you today as you begin this journey is simple:

Receive it.

Swim in it.

Begin to believe it.

Day 2

He thinks about you all the time. If you could collect each thought in your hands and count them – it would be like trying count the grains of sand on the beach. *So, you couldn't if you tried.*

And what type of thoughts does He think? He says they are *precious and rare.* Every one of these thoughts, are loving, deep and beautiful. Every. Single. One.

So even on your worst day, His thoughts of you are precious. Do you believe it? I'm praying it digs down deep in your soul today.

How precious are your thoughts about me, O God. They cannot be numbered! I can't even count them; They outnumber the grains of sand! And when I wake up, you are still with me!

Psalm 139: 17,18

Day 3

You have probably heard it said, *"God doesn't make junk."* But, do you believe that you are made:

W onderfully & Fearfully

These are the words penned by David, a man after God's heart. In fact, he goes on to say, God took great detail in making you. *He made you distinct and marvelous.* You, walking around in your fuzzy slippers or wearing your favorite pair of red shoes – *you inspire awe.*

And while you're at it, if you go back to the very beginning, when the world was new, you can read His opinion of all that He made on day 1:

Then God looked over all he had made, and he saw that it was very good! (Genesis 1:31)

And the truth is – He is still making good things. Wonderful things. And yes, not junk.

I will give thanks to You, for I am fearfully and wonderfully made; wonderful are Your works, And my soul knows it very well.

Psalm 139:14 (New American Standard)

Do you know it?

Very well? You are made fearfully and wonderfully.

That is what He said, anyway.

Day 4

O Lord, you have examined my heart and know {Yada}
everything about me.

Psalm 139:1

Yada :: {Hebrew} to know by experience, to understand, to be acquainted with

He thinks about you all the time... He made you wonderfully.... It would stand to reason, *that He knows you*. He knows your heart, *even the parts you keep hidden from your BFF*. He knows where you are going and where you have been. He even knows what you are thinking and what you are going to say next.

The Hebrew word for "know" is *Yada. He knows. Jehovah Yada. The One True God, knows you.*

I know what you are thinking, *"Yada, yada, yada" "Blah, blah, blah" — so?* Our culture has taken the meaning of this word and turned it into casual conversation worthy of a sitcom. *Yah. Yah. Yah. I know. I know. I know.*

But, Jehovah Yada. He knows you. *Deep down in your gut – He knows you.* He gets you. He is acquainted with ALL your ways. And with all this knowing He desires a relationship with you.

So hug your knees tight, close your eyes and let that truth meet you right where you are.

He knows you. No need for pretending. No masks required. Yada. Yada. Yada.

Day 5

Deep and wide, deep and wide there's a fountain flowing deep and wide. Deep and wide, deep and wide, there's a fountain flowing deep and wide.

As Sunday school songs go, this was never my favorite. We would stand in front of our chairs while Bonita played it on the old upright piano. Taking our little hands we would mark out the deep and then the wide and smile. *I don't think I really knew, at age seven, what the fountain was or what was flowing so wide and deep inside it.*

In the 1980s I sang *Love is a Battlefield* with sky-high over-permed hair while wearing my favorite pink fluorescent shirt and acid washed jeans. It certainly felt true at sixteen, when I wasn't pretty enough or popular enough to have a class ring wrapped in yarn around my finger.

Today I read these words...

And may you have the power to understand, as all God's people should, how wide, how long, how high, and how deep his love is. May you experience the love of Christ, though it is too great to understand fully. (Ephesians 3:18)

I smile, because now I know what is flowing deep and wide in the fountain. *Does He really love me like that? Does His love really flow for me?*

Suddenly, I remember standing on the beach watching

my girls dive into the water. They are overwhelmed by the waves, giggling mermaids, and I am smitten with them. He leans in close and says, *"Yes, I love you like that. Like children playing in the ocean deep, like waves that keep coming and coming and coming—my love for you is too big, too fantastic for you to even begin to understand. But you can dive deep, you can play in the waves, and you can believe it."*

And I remember another Sunday school song...

I've got love like an ocean, I've got love like an ocean, I've got love like an ocean in my soul... Maybe I'll teach it to my little mermaids today. Care to sing along? *You are loved like an ocean.* Do you know it?

Copyright Information for "What God Wants You to Know:"

What God Wants You To Know is available as a free gift when you subscribe to my 29 Lincoln Avenue monthly(ish) newsletter. To find out more information go to:

http://www.29lincolnavenue.com/subscribe-to-my-newsletter/

Made in the USA
San Bernardino, CA
17 April 2014